Home Before Dark

or The Saga of Miss Edie Hill

A play

Jimmie Chinn

Samuel French – London
New York – Toronto – Hollywood

ISBN 0 573 01787 5

Please see pages v and vi for further copyright information

HOME BEFORE DARK
or
The Saga of Miss Edie Hill

First presented by Youth Action Theatre at Hampton Court Theatre on 13 March, 1993 with the following cast:

Edie Hill	Catherine Early
Alfie	Peter Gardiner
Doris Fitton	Christine Osborne
Betty Bowkley	Sarah Jane Renton
Joyce Tattershall	Fiona McMahon
Irish Mary	Alice Langrish
Dad	David Hannigan
Percy Tully	William Allen
Eric Schofield	Robbie Frater
Johnny Mulligan	John Addley
Sean Mulligan	Alex Stringer
Mick Mulligan	George Scott
Miss Keegan	Joanna Viney
Maurice Huggins	Simon Josolyne
Daft Lizzie	Sarah Mounds
Alan Tweedale	Miles Hawkins
Peggy Grant	Lisa Nagle
Hettie Turner	Caroline Chown
Joan Moss	Jo Kentish
Eileen Sparks	Emma Donaghy
Marlene Tibbs	Catherine Barrs
Hilda Grey	Marilese Reid
Lydia Bracewell	Daisy Hughes
Abe	Damon McCollin-Moore
Buzz	David Chouvin
Tommy Hill	Nairn McCrudden
Rita	Georgina Carter
Patrick Kelly	Ben Fricke
George Field	Mark Crossland

Other roles played by members of the company

Directed by Eric Yardley and Rick de Kerckhove
Production design by Christine Osborne
Lighting by Simon Roose

CHARACTERS

Edie Hill
Alfie, her younger brother
Doris Fitton
Betty Bowkley
Joyce Tattershall
Irish Mary
Dad
Percy Tully
Eric Schofield
Johnny Mulligan
Sean Mulligan
Mick Mulligan
Miss Keegan
Maurice Huggins
Daft Lizzie
Alan Tweedale
Peggy Grant
Hettie Turner
Joan Moss
Eileen Sparks
Marlene Tibbs
Hilda Grey
Lydia Bracewell
Abe
Buzz
Tommy Hill, Edie's son
Rita
Bearers, Pub Customers, Salvation Army Members, Wedding Guests, Train Passengers and Porter, Extras

The action takes place in a small cotton mill town in Lancashire

Time—the eighteen years spanning from 1946 to 1964

ACT I

The action begins in 1946

A bare stage with a bed and doorframe to represent Edie's bedroom

In the darkness Gracie Fields sings "Sally"

A pool of light comes up around the bed—in it is Edie who, with her knees up under the cover, is about to give birth. She screams out in agony and sweat pours from her brow. She calls for help but no-one is to hand. It must be pointed out that although Edie might be seen from time to time as a tragic figure, she is also essentially very funny

Edie (*calling, in pain, sweating profusely*) Oh, bloody hell, somebody . . . Help! . . . Help, somebody . . . I'm having a baby here . . .!

Alfie, who will from time to time act as narrator, steps into the light beside the bed. He is dressed as a boy of thirteen, short trousers, pullover with holes, braces, etc.

Alfie (*to the audience; always cheerful, every smiling; in his adult voice*)
This is the saga of Miss Edie Hill,
Little and tough, who worked in a mill.

Edie (*almost overlapping*) Oh, God! . . . It's no joke is this . . . I'm in agony here . . . Help me, please . . . Please help me . . .!

Alfie (*to the audience*)
Brought herself up without any mother,
Looked after Dad and Alfie, her brother. (*He points to himself with a cheeky grin*)

Edie (*calling*) Alfie! Typical. Never here when you want him . . . Alfie!

Alfie She asked for nowt and that's just what she got,
But why complain? That was her lot!

Loud banging on a door as another pool of light comes up on three of Edie's friends: Doris, Betty and Joyce dressed as mill girls in overalls, turbans or headscarfs and clogs or boots

Doris (*banging on a street door; calling*) Edie . . . ? Edie, whatever's to do in there?

Alfie She worked at a loom for most of her life,
A wonderful mother but nobody's wife!

Betty (*also knocking; calling*) Edie, love . . . it's Betty and Doris and Joyce . . . whatever's up?

Alfie On that day long ago—screaming in bed,
She gave birth to Tommy, but they thought he was dead.

Joyce Break down the door, for God's sake—she sounds in pain in there!

Alfie "Hang on", said Tommy, "look—I'm breathing!",
And by the look in his eye you could tell he was seething!

Betty Come on, let's give it a shove.

Betty, Doris and Joyce lean heavily against the door

Alfie In time she lost Dad, and her brother died, too,
And with Tommy to feed—what could she do?

The door falls to the floor as Doris, Betty and Joyce rush to the bed

Alfie (*walking across to the fallen door*)
And that is the story we'll tell you tonight,
You'll laugh and you'll cry but it's full of delight,
'Cos travel the globe and you never will,
Meet another living soul like our Edie Hill! (*He waits in the shadows by the fallen door*)

Doris (*at the bed*) Edie, what's wrong?

Betty (*lowering her voice*) I think she's passed out.

Joyce How can she have passed out? Talk sense, Betty. She's moaning and groaning.

Doris She's not dying, is she? She might be—you never know.

Betty Oh, don't say that, Doris. Should we fetch a doctor? What d'you think?

Joyce Hang on—I'll ask her. (*To Edie*) Edie, love, are you dying or what? Only we're very worried here.

Edie (*half in agony, half in temper*) Course I'm not bloody dying—fetch towels and boiling water.

Doris (*to the others*) What does she want towels and boiling water for?

Edie Don't just stand there, you willy buggers—I'm having a baby . . . Now! (*She gives one final push as she screams out*)

Betty She's what?
Joyce Take no notice—you know Edie—she's always being fanciful.
Doris She'll have seen it on the pictures—you know what she's like.
Betty (*loudly*) Pull yourself together, Edie Hill—we know what you're up to.
Joyce Pulling our legs—she's always doing that.

Alfie appears by the fallen door

Alfie What's goin' on? Who's broken our door down? Me dad'll go mad!
Doris Clear off, Alfie. Your Edie's having a fit.
Alfie Oh, yes. I've heard that before. She'll be havin' you on—you know what she's like.
Joyce You're a heartless little sod, you! She could be dying here for all you care.

Betty lifts the covers and is pale and horrified

Betty Oh, my God!
Doris (*seeing her face, thunderstruck*) What is it, Betty? Betty, what is it?
Betty (*screaming to Alfie, urgently*) Alfie, quick! Go at once and fetch Irish Mary . . .!
Alfie What for?
Betty Just do as you're told. Tell her to come at once!
Alfie (*now in panic*) I'm not sure where she lives.
Betty Number two, Back of Beyond—tell her to get her bloody skates on.
Alfie But I don't like her—she scares me!
Doris (*going to Alfie, hitting him round the earhole*) Just do as Betty tells you and get gone!
Alfie (*holding his ear*) Just wait till me dad gets home—I'll tell him you hit me.
Doris (*chasing him off*) Hit you! I'll knock you soddin' senseless, you marred bugger!
Alfie (*running into the shadows*) Just you wait, Doris Fitton—my dad'll blind you when I tell him . . .!

Alfie "exits" running (round the stage)

Joyce (*to Betty*) It's not a baby, is it, Betty? A real baby?
Betty Well, it's not a meat pudding, Joyce. Look.

Joyce (*turning away*) Oh, I daren't. I don't like babies.

Doris (*back at the bed*) What a turn up, eh? I didn't even know she was expecting, did you?

Betty Well, she's never said anythin' to me. Joyce?

Joyce (*hiding her face*) What?

Betty Did you know about this?

Joyce How would I know? She'd never tell me. You're supposed to be her very best friend, Betty Bowkley.

Edie (*coming to*) Where am I? What's happened?

Betty (*comforting Edie*) It's all right, love. You've had a bit of a turn—that's all.

Edie What about the baby—where's me baby?

Doris (*looking under the covers, ashen, whispering to Betty and Joyce*) It's dead. . . . I'm sure it's dead.

Alfie, who has run round the stage, breathless, holding his ear and crying with rage, bumps into Irish Mary, a dirty, gipsy-type irish woman with dyed red hair and curlers. She wears boots, probably a man's, not quite laced up properly

Irish Mary (*stopping him*) What in heaven's name's wrong wi' you . . . is the devil after you or what?

Alfie (*holding his nose because she smells*) You've got to come . . . you've got to come now, Irish Mary. It's our Edie . . . she's having a fit!

Irish Mary A fit? What kind of a fit is she having, lad?

Alfie I'm not sure . . . she's got her legs in the air, an' she's screamin' and sweatin' . . .

Irish Mary That sounds like a fit all right . . .

Alfie An' Doris Fitton an' Betty Bowkley an' Joyce Tattershall have broke our door down an' me dad'll go mad—an' Doris Fitton clouted me round the earhole!

Irish Mary Yes, well, you probably asked for it——

Alfie You've got to get your skates on.

Irish Mary Ay, well, tell 'em I'm on me way . . .

Alfie, still holding his nose, exits running. Irish Mary follows him, blowing her nose on her dirty apron

Edie Have you done anything—have you sent for somebody? Not me dad, whatever you do—he mustn't know about this or he'll kill me . . .

Betty (*putting her arm around Edie*) Shhh, now, love—shhh. It'll be all right.

Joyce We've sent for Irish Mary, love. She's had thirteen of her own—she'll know what to do.

Edie I don't want her here—smellin' the house out. Cut it free—that's what you do, Betty—cut it free. (*She tries to look under the covers*)

Betty (*preventing her from looking*) Don't look, Edie. Not yet—don't look, love.

Edie Is it a boy? I've always imagined it being a boy.

Betty I can't tell what it is, love. It looks like a rabbit if you ask me.

Joyce If it's a boy it'll have a little do-dah. I thought everybody knew that!

Doris Joyce—just shut it, will you. We all know what little boys have—that's what's the cause of all this bloody lark!

Joyce (*always prim*) Oh, you're dirty minded, Doris Fitton. You know I didn't mean *that*!

Alfie runs on from round the corner, out of breath. He is followed by Irish Mary, also breathless

Alfie (*at the fallen door*) I've fetched her . . . and she doesn't half pong!

Irish Mary (*hitting him round the other ear*) Don't you be personal, young man. (*Out of breath*) Holy Mother of God—I'm past all this runnin'.

Doris (*going to Mary*) You'd better be quick, Mrs Mulligan—I think it's serious.

Irish Mary What's ailing the child? I'm no doctor, you know.

Joyce (*bringing her to the bed, lowering her voice*) It's a baby. She's given birth, but we think it's dead.

Irish Mary The Lord save us—the poor little bugger!

Irish Mary, Doris, Betty and Joyce crowd round the bed to obscure Edie from our sight

Alfie (*from the door, trying to get a glance*) A baby? Did somebody say a baby? We haven't ordered a baby, have we?

Doris (*from the bed area*) Unless you want another good hiding you best get shifted, Alfie Hill.

Alfie Has our Edie had a baby?

Irish Mary (*firing instructions*) Get some boilin' water . . . and two or three clean towels . . . and somebody go to the call box and ring Doctor Hempling.

Alfie (*to the audience; in his grown-up voice*)
I listened and listened to all of this talk,
I even looked up expecting a stork,
All right, so I don't know what happens to ladies,
But I know it's a fact that it's him who brings babies!
(*He winks and smiles*)
And not being sure about a girl or a lad,
I ran down to the mill to inform my dad!

Dad comes round the corner in flat cap and overalls

Alfie runs to him and holds his hand

Alfie (*shouting as he comes to the house*) You've all had it now 'cos me dad's here!

Edie Oh, hell, no! Not me dad! He'll kill me, Betty!

As the women round the bed step aside they reveal Edie now sitting up and looking tired but much brighter. Irish Mary, sleeves rolled up and looking as if she'd just done a day's washing, wipes the sweat from her brow. Betty is holding a bowl of steaming water, Doris is holding a couple of soiled and bloody towels, and Joyce, looking petrified, is holding something wrapped in a towel

Dad stands looking at the fallen door, bewildered, holding Alfie's hand

Dad (*looking at the door*) What the hell's going on?

Alfie There she is, Dad—it's Doris Fitton who hit me.

Dad What're you lot doin' here? And I've told you about that mad Irish sod—I don't want her in my house!

Irish Mary Is that all the thanks I get for saving your daughter's life? May God forgive you, Alfred Hill.

Dad Edie . . . what's goin' on round here?

Betty Come on, Edie. Get it over with. Tell him.

Edie Promise you won't hit me, Dad. Promise you won't strike me. I couldn't help it—honest!

Dad Is it an accident?

Edie (*fearful but funny*) Well, it is an accident . . . yes, sort of.

Dad Have you been knocked down—run over—what?

Doris Tell him, Edie. Tell him and get it over with.

Edie I've had a baby, Dad.

Dad (*incredulous; to Irish Mary*) What's she on about?

Irish Mary You're not deaf, are you, as well as daft? You heard what the girl said . . . she's just given birth . . . about three weeks too early, I'd say.

Dad But . . . but, I don't understand. How did that happen?

Irish Mary Well, if you don't know *that* by now I'm not the one to be after telling you!

Dad I didn't know she was expecting—she never told me.

Betty She never told any of us, Mr Hill.

Doris You must know your Edie by now, Mr Hill. She's always lived in a world of her own.

Dad (*his temper flashing; going for Edie*) Why, you dirty, stupid little . . .!

Irish Mary, with the strength of ten men, grabs hold of Dad's upheld fists and prevents him getting to Edie, who looks scared

Irish Mary You so much as touch that poor girl and I'll smash your filthy Protestant face in!

Dad You stay out of this, you dirty Irish mare!

Alfie (*over-excited by all this*) Go on, Dad—bash her-bash her—then bash Doris Fitton!

Edie (*tears running down her face; commanding attention*) Just stop it! Stop it all of you!

Betty Edie, love, calm down.

Edie What does it all matter anyway? The baby's dead, isn't it? (*She weeps*)

Joyce (*still holding the bundle in a towel, looking petrified*) It isn't, you know. Whatever this thing is it isn't dead—it's moving and it's breathing!

Black-out

The actors exit

The sound of a baby crying. Immediately a pool of light comes up DL

Alfie walks into the light. He is cheerful and smiling

Alfie (*aside*) I've heard it said that life is strange,
And best leave things for God to arrange.
But who'd have thought, me an uncle, our Edie a mother,
And her—with one leg shorter than t'other . . .

A pool of Light comes up c *on Edie, now dressed as a child. We now see for the first time that she has a slight club foot on which she wears a special shoe. She stands in her light, sucking a lollipop and looking innocent but cheeky*

That's her now on her first day at school,
And even at that age she was nobody's fool.

The Lights come up on a school playground and Edie is joined by Doris, Betty and Joyce, also schoolgirls now. Doris is skipping with a rope. Betty, who is sucking a stick of rock, walks around Edie looking down at her foot, intrigued

Doris (*skipping*) One potato, two potato, three potato, four . . . five potato, six potato, seven potato more . . .

Joyce Come on, Doris Fitton, it's my turn now. You've had more than a five minute go.

Doris (*skipping*) Drop dead!

Joyce Oh, you'll have a baby now. My mum says that little girls who use bad language always end up having babies—so there!

Doris Your mum's a prostitute anyway . . . six potato, seven potato . . . (*she continues*)

Joyce Oh, that's a lie. Anyway—what's a prostitute? Your dad's a prostitute!

Betty (*intrigued*) What's the matter with your foot?

Edie What d'you want to know for?

Betty You walk with a limp, don't you? I've seen you.

Edie It's only pretend. It's so as I don't have to do P.T. with Mrs Butterworth.

Betty You lucky thing. She makes you tuck your vest in your knickers and all the boys say rude things.

Edie There you are then. I'm lucky. And I can go on the cripples' outing to Blackpool. You can, see, when you limp.

Betty I'd like a shoe like that. Then I could go to Blackpool.

Joyce (*to Doris*) Anyway, I'm not playing with you, Doris Fitton. (*She cries*)

Betty (*to Joyce*) What's up with you now? You're always skricking.

Joyce She called my mam a prostitute.

Doris (*stopping skipping*) Oh, Joyce Tattershall, I did no such thing.

Joyce Oh, yes, you did!

Doris Oh, no, I did not!

Joyce (*to Betty and Edie*) What is a prostitute anyway?

Edie We've got a woman in our street and she's one of them.

Betty Really! What's she look like?

Edie She's got red hair and she's Irish and she has a new baby every month.

Joyce I expect she swears all the time—that's why she keeps having babies.

Edie My mam just had a baby and she never swore.

Betty Hey, did you watch and see where it came from? It comes out of your bum, doesn't it?

Joyce Oh, Betty Bowkley, wash your mouth out this minute!

Edie Anyway, my mam went to Heaven to get our Alfie.

Betty That's stupid. Anybody who goes to Heaven never comes back.

Edie She didn't.

Joyce How d'you mean?

Edie She sent my baby brother but my dad said she liked it so much in Heaven that's why she stayed there.

Doris (*who has been listening*) Have you been—to Heaven?

Edie 'Course not. But I could if I wanted. It's my foot see—it makes you very special having a bad foot, my dad says.

Joyce How do you get one?

Edie You're either born with it or, like me, you have to have infantile paralysis and when you get better your foot's gone all numb.

Joyce (*wide-eyed*) And it makes you special?

Edie Very. (*She sucks her lolly, secretly pleased with herself that they're being taken in by all this*)

Joyce Hey, can I be your friend?

Betty And me.

Edie I'll think about it and let you know.

Betty Thanks.

Joyce Thanks, Edith.

Edie And you can call me Edie if you like.

Betty and Joyce look at each other in delight and both walk away limping like Edie

Edie (*winking at Doris, who is still skipping*) They're daft, them two—they'll believe anything you tell 'em.

Fade to Light DL *on Alfie*

Alfie So Doris and Betty and Joyce in the end,
Knew clearly why Edie was their 'special' friend.
What did it matter to walk on one side?
At least she was honest, with nothing to hide.

A pool of Light comes up on Edie, back in bed, breastfeeding her child

Things settled down—and so did me dad,
Who had to admit that things weren't so bad,
Edie had Tommy with barely a ripple,
And all Tommy needed was my sister's nipple!

Alfie's Light fades as he walks away into the darkness beyond

A warm glow now surrounds the bed

Dad enters and sees Edie

Dad (*turning to go again*) Oh, I'm sorry, Edie. I should have knocked.

Edie (*doing up her blouse*) Don't be daft, Dad. I've got to feed him.

Dad Ay, but it's private.

Edie You're not embarrassed, surely to goodness?

Dad (*clearly embarrassed*) No, no . . . I'm not embarrassed.

Edie You must have seen Mam feeding me.

Dad No. No, I never did. It's not a man's place to see all that.

Edie Oh, you are old-fashioned, Dad. Come on—come and sit down.

Dad (*sitting on a chair beside her bed*) He's lookin' grand. What will you call him?

Edie (*smiling*) Mistake, I think. That's what he is. I suppose you'd call him Shock.

Dad Ay, well. Not to worry. I'm getting quite used to him. (*Peering into the shawl*) He's bonny, I'll give him that.

Edie He favours Mam. Don't you think?

Dad How can you tell that? He's not proper formed yet.

Edie (*tears welling up in her eyes*) I love him, Dad. I thought I wouldn't. I even tried to get rid of him before he was born.

Dad Well, I'm glad you didn't. (*An awkward pause*) I've got to ask you, love—who was he? Who was the father?

Edie (*wiping her eyes*) I'm not telling you, Dad. Please—you mustn't ask me.

Dad But it's not right, love. Why should he get away with it? He has a responsibility here.

Edie I'm not interested. Anyway, he wouldn't care even if I told him.

Dad You mean you haven't?

Edie No. Why should I, Dad? I've told you—he'd run a mile.

Dad But a child needs a dad, Edie. Specially a lad. Who'll take him to football—who'll play with his train set?

Edie He's got you. He's got our Alfie. What more will he want?

Dad It's you I worry about. You've had no life. You've looked after me and our Alfie.

Edie So what? You looked after both of us when Mam died in childbirth. I've only done what anybody would have done.

Dad Not anybody, love. You. You're a good person. You're like she was. She was a good person.

Edie I wish she was here now. She'd have loved him. (*She looks down at the baby*)

Dad Yes, well, she's not here and we've got to make things right. How will you manage?

Edie I shall carry on at the mill. I've got to.

Dad There's no need for that. We can manage on what I bring home.

Edie No, Dad. Thanks all the same. But I've made up my mind . . . I was daft enough to have him so I must look after him. I'll carry on working and I'll find somebody to have him during the day.

Dad Who? Not Irish Mary, for God's sake!

Edie No fear. Anyhow, she's enough of her own to bother about. We'll find someone. (*To the baby*) Won't we, Tommy?

Dad (*smiling*) Oh, so it's Tommy then?

Edie Why not? It's good enough.

They both smile at each other. Music

The stage becomes a school playground as Edie exits with Dad

As many of the cast as possible enter as school kids, boys in short pants, girls in gym-slips, hair ribbons, etc. Like an army the kids set about transforming the bed and the fallen door into a brick wall and a slide (or similar). Other kids play hopscotch, football, skipping, etc. They all sing as they work

Children (*singing*) The big ship sails on the Ally-Ally O,
The Ally-Ally O,
The Ally-Ally O.
Yes, the big ship sails on the Ally-Ally O,
On the last day of September . . .

Alfie (*aside, over the music*) There was only one school at the end of our street,
And before the bell sounded it's here that we'd meet,
Shelley and Cleggy and Harry and Dick,
The Mulligans, Johnny and Sean and another called Mick.
They were all Irish Mary's and as scruffy as her,
And how could you miss 'em—they all had red hair!
The boy over there, that's him on the end,
He's called Eric Schofield and I call him my friend.
The trouble with Eric, he's got a weak chest,
A fact that's made worse by the holes in his vest.
He has to take tablets and breathe through a tube,
And that flask contains beef tea made from a cube.
That tall lad's a bugger—he's called Percy Tully,
He's got a big willy and, that's right, he's a bully!

Percy (*calling; to Alfie*) Hey! You! Short-arse!

The singing stops and everyone freezes. They are all terrified of Tully the bully

Alfie quickly joins Eric Schofield, who wears thick glasses and carries a thermos flask at all times

Alfie (*to Eric*) Here, I think he's talking to you, Eric.
Eric (*terrified, cowering behind Alfie*) He's not, is he?
Percy (*calling again*) You I'm talking to, No-Dick!
Alfie You see—it's definitely you he wants, Eric.
Eric I'll get me mam on to him at home time.
Alfie An' I'll get our Edie—she'll blind him!
Percy (*coming across, grabbing Alfie by the back of the neck*) It's you I'm talking to, Scragend!
Alfie (*in pain*) You're a mad git, you. Gerroff!
Percy What did you call me, Short-arse?
Alfie You're hurtin' me, Tully! I'll get our Edie on to you—she'll stick one on you—just you wait.
Percy Oh, yes? Her and whose army?
Alfie Anyway, I'm an uncle now so I don't need anybody to stick up for me.
Percy You're a what, Short-arse?
Eric He's an uncle, see—so put that in your mouth and suck it, Tully!

Percy Just shut it, Schofield—unless you want me to put your tablets down the lav like last time.

Eric (*still cowering behind Alfie*) Well, he is an uncle, so there.

Percy An uncle. What, Alfie Anthill an uncle. How can you be an uncle at your age?

Alfie It's true. Our Edie's had a baby, see. She got it last week.

Percy What—got it through the post, did she? Through the soddin' letter box!

The rest of the kids laugh

I bet you don't even know how a kid is got, do you, Short-arse?

Alfie Yes, I do. I know all about it, Tully. You sit in a very hot bath and drink gin.

Percy Cobblers!

More laughter from the children

Alfie Oh yes you do. Our Edie was doing that all the time—I saw her.

Percy And where's the dad, then? Since when has your Edie been married?

Alfie She's not married. Why should she be married?

Percy That shows you how much you know. You've got to be married to get a baby, see. Tosspot!

The three Mulligan boys, Johnny, Sean and Mick, each with red hair, pipe up now

Johnny That's not true, Tully.

Sean That's right—our mam's got thirteen of us and she's not married.

Percy Well, your mam's a Catholic, in't she? It doesn't count with Catholics. You don't have to be married 'cos your dad's the Pope, in't he?

The three Mulligan boys look at each other and say together, puzzled, "Is he?"

Mick There's a picture of him on our wall but I didn't know he was our dad!

Percy (*punching Alfie's arm*) Anyroad, I know what I'm talkin' about, Anthill—an' you've got to be wed or you can't get a baby—an' you've got to be fifty to be an uncle, right, Tosspot?

Miss Keegan enters. She is stern and strict in a two-piece suit and glasses. She blows a whistle long and loud

Everyone freezes

Percy Here, hang on, miss—it's too early for the whistle.
Miss Keegan I beg your pardon, my watch is spot on!
Johnny It's not fair, miss.
Miss Keegan Life isn't fair, Johnny Mulligan. I hope you haven't been bullying again, Percival Tully.
Percy (*with his hands in his pockets*) Bullying, miss? What, me?
Miss Keegan Alfred Hill—tell the truth now—has Percival Tully been bullying you?

Percy looks at Alfie threateningly

Alfie (*seeing Percy*) No, Miss Keegan.
Miss Keegan Honestly?
Alfie (*his head bent*) No, Miss Keegan. I mean yes, Miss Keegan.
Miss Keegan And you, Eric Schofield. Has Percival Tully been bullying you?
Eric Yes, miss. And he tipped my tablets down the toilet and flushed it. I might die now.
Miss Keegan I thought as much. I suspected it. I'm warning you here and now, Tully, that if I so much as catch you anywhere near those two boys you'll be bending for the Headmaster! (*She blows her whistle*) Single file!

All the kids form a single line facing left

(*Another short blast on the whistle*) Off we go—into the hall.

The kids move round the stage in a circle, singing as they go, and then come to rest cross-legged on the floor in a semi-circle

The Lights change to indicate the school hall

Children (*singing*) Jesus loves the little children,
All the children of the world,
Red or yellow, black or white,
They are precious in His sight,
Jesus loves the little children of the world.

Sean (*holding his hand up*) Miss . . . please, miss.

Miss Keegan Yes, Sean Mulligan—what is it?

Sean Please, miss—there aren't any yellow kids, are there, miss?

Miss Keegan Of course there are: in far off China and Japan and Egypt—just as there are black folk in Togo-Togo Land.

Mick (*to Sean*) Where's that?

Percy I saw a black person once, miss. Our dog went for him.

Miss Keegan Please—can we get down to our arithmetic?

Johnny (*holding his hand up*) Can I ask you a question, please, miss?

Miss Keegan If it isn't a silly question, yes, you may.

Johnny You're not married, are you, miss?

Miss Keegan I am not. Hence why you must address me at all times as "miss".

Alfie Does that mean you can't have a baby, miss?

Percy (*hitting Eric*) She's past it anyway, silly old bat!

Miss Keegan What an extremely rude and impertinent question, Alfred Hill. Wash your mouth out at once!

Sean Percy Tully says that you can only get a baby if you're married, miss.

Miss Keegan You're all far too young to know about such things. When you're twenty-one will be soon enough to learn about the birds and the bees.

Mick What've the birds and bees got to do with it, miss?

Miss Keegan Can we kindly proceed with the lesson, please?

Johnny Alfie Hill says he's an uncle, miss. How come?

Miss Keegan Alfie Hill is in the very unfortunate position to have a wicked sister who, like most of you by the sounds of it, was in too much of a hurry to taste the fruits of lust.

Percy What's that, miss? What's lust?

Miss Keegan (*blushing*) Your books open, please. Page twenty-two. Multiplication! (*She blushes even more*)

Black-out

As the Children exit they make noises to simulate the sounds of a cotton mill: spinning frames, etc.

The Lights come up DR*on the ladies' lavatory at the mill. The sounds of the mill gradually fade*

Edie, Betty and Doris enter

Betty (*excited, secretive*) Come on, Edie—let's have it then.

Edie (*fishing in her overall pocket and bringing out an airmail letter*) Give us a chance, Betty. It's here somewhere.

Doris (*lighting three Woodbines*) Keep an eye out for Joyce—we don't want her finding out.

Betty (*tearing the letter open*) Oh, I'm dead excited. I'm nearly wetting meself here.

Edie Me dad's getting very suspicious—strange letters arriving at our house. (*She takes a fag from Doris*)

Betty Well, I couldn't give Abe my address, Edie, could I? Me dad'll kill me. (*She takes a fag from Doris*)

Edie Well, if you two will get mixed up with American G.I.s . . .

Doris Just read the flippin' letter, Betty.

Betty (*reading*) "Dear Dolories and Gloria . . ."

Edie (*screaming with laughter*) Dolories . . . Gloria!

Betty Well, we couldn't give 'em our real names, could we?

Edie Which one's which?

Doris She's Dolories—I'm Gloria. Now just read the letter, Betty.

Betty Hey, kid, just listen to this: (*She reads*) "Dear Dolories and Gloria, Just a line to say that Buzz and I are home safely in the good old U.S. of A. and thinking of you both every hour of every day. Life sure is lonesome without you——"

Doris We only met them twice!

Betty "The two nights we spent together in Warrington were simply fabulous—especially for two homesick G.I.s like us. And listen, you guys, I want a letter and a photo from you, Dolories, and Buzz sure wants the same from Gloria. We enclose snapshots of us—sealed with love and kisses——"

Edie (*grabbing for the two photographs*) Here—let's have a look!

Doris (*fear in her eyes, getting hold of them first*) Hands off, Edie—they belong to us!

Edie (*surprised but trying to hide it*) Oh, well—please yourselves.

Betty "Don't forget now, one of these days we'll be back in Lancashire to drag you two up the aisle—a double wedding, eh, girls?" (*Her hands shaking, almost crying*) Hey, Doris—they want to marry us!

Doris (*just as overcome*) The cheeky buggers!

Their enthusiasm and their naïvety is quite touching

Edie You don't believe all that rubbish, I hope?

Betty Shurrup—you're only jealous, Edie Hill!

Edie The war's over long since—they won't be back!

Doris How does it end, Betty?

Betty "Don't forget to write now and send the photographs—we both need you under our pillows! A parcel is on its way to you—nylons, chewing-gum and Hershey bars! Our deepest love and affection, Abe and Buzz." . . . and (*she counts*) twelve kisses, Doris!

Joyce enters

Joyce Here, what's going on? Huggins is looking for you three.

Betty (*handing the letter to Doris*) Get rid of that—and the photos!

Doris I'll put 'em in my knickers. They'll be safe there. (*She does so*)

Joyce What are they? Come on, show us.

Edie It's not for you, Joyce.

Joyce It's something to do with . . . (*lowering her voice*) sex, I suppose.

Betty Never you mind.

Joyce I don't care anyway. I'm going to be like my mam: have nothing to do with . . . you-know-what!

Doris Come off it, Joyce. Even your mother must have had it *once* to get you.

Joyce Yes, but she's never bothered with it since.

Betty How do *you* know?

Joyce She told me. "Joyce", she said, "it's so long since your dad and me did it, I've forgotten what it's like."

The other three girls laugh

Anyway—what do we know about it? We know nothin'.

Betty (*winking at Doris*) We know a bit, don't we, Doris?

Edie Joyce's right. What do we know about all that?

Doris Come off it, Edie. You've had a baby. You didn't get that picking your nose!

They laugh and smoke

Maurice Huggins, the gaffer, walks in carrying a clip-board and pencil to denote his status

Maurice Ay, ay—what's all this then?

Edie Do you mind? This is the Ladies'!

Betty Surely we can have a pee and a swallow (*the cigarette*) in peace.

Maurice It's not a flippin' holiday camp, you know. All your ends are down out there.

Doris They're always down. That's what we're paid for, isn't it? To piece 'em up again.

Edie Paid for, did you say? I'd hardly call three pound a week being paid.

Maurice If you don't like it, you know what you can do. There's always the dole.

Doris Anyway, that Egyptian cotton's awful. It's like trying to spin candy floss.

Maurice If you've got any complaints, see Mr Tweedale.

Edie What good would that do? He lives up there on Tangle Hill with that stuck-up son of his and couldn't care less about skivvies like us. How does he expect anybody to live on three pound?

Maurice You've a lot to say for yourself just lately.

Betty She's got another mouth to feed now, you know.

Joyce My friend Sadie Greenhalgh told me she gets three pound ten shillings up at Cawley and Cunliffe's.

Maurice Well, you know where it is. Number fifty-nine bus outside—go and get a job there. You won't be allowed a sly fag every five minutes at Cawley and Cunliffe's . . . sweated labour up there.

Doris And this place is not, you mean? We'd be better off dead, Maurice Huggins, we would!

Maurice You will be if you don't get back in there and attend to your frames.Now, let's be havin' you.

Muttering, the four girls put out their fags and exit

Maurice detains Edie

Maurice How's the little lad then?

Edie He's none of your business.

Maurice I'm only askin'.

Edie Well, don't. He'll never go short as long as I can work in this hell-hole!

Maurice Who looks after him while you're at work?

Edie Our Alfie's on summer holiday from school—he can manage.

Maurice And when he's back at school?

Edie I'll find somebody.

Maurice That'll cost you. Folk don't mind kids for nowt, you know.

Edie Look, Maurice, I've told you once—stay out of my business.

Edie limps away and exits

Maurice smiles to himself

Music as the Lights cross-fade to bright sunshine and the sounds of birds and kids playing and laughing at a distance

Alfie enters wheeling a big, old-fashioned pram with the baby inside it

Alfie (*aside*) Somehow the summers seemed much longer then,
A few weeks at school and we'd break up again.
But it suited me dad, and our Edie too,
'Cos I could wheel Tommy out and show him the view.
I'd sit on the Rec where the other kids played,
And if the sun was too hot, we'd sit in the shade.
No life for a lad, but I was happy enough,
Even though Tully said I'd end up a puff.

Daft Lizzie wanders on as he speaks to us. She comes over to the pram and looks in it

But then something happened that summer up there,
A woman called Lizzie, with long straggly hair,
Came over and parked herself right next to me,
She looked in the pram and said——

Daft Lizzie (*being deaf, she speaks loudly with ill-formed words*) Is it a baby?

Alfie (*to Daft Lizzie*) You what?

Daft Lizzie I say, is it a baby? I'll bet it's a baby.

Alfie Course it's a baby.

Daft Lizzie Is it yours? I say, is it yours?

Alfie Course it's not mine. I'm too young to have a baby. It's me sister's.

Daft Lizzie (*reading his lips*) You what?

Alfie (*mouthing the words clearly*) My sister's. Our Edie's lad.

Daft Lizzie I know her. We went to school together once.

Alfie I know. You're Daft Lizzie, aren't you?

Daft Lizzie I can't hear. I'm deaf, see.

Alfie And you're daft. Everybody knows that.

Daft Lizzie I like babies. I looked after me little brother—but he died.

Alfie Why did he die?

Daft Lizzie He was afflicted. Couldn't breathe proper.
Alfie Why was that?
Daft Lizzie It was the cotton that killed him. Me mam used to take him to the mill. No good, see. All that cotton dust.
Alfie She could have had more sense.
Edie (*off; calling, worried*) Alfie . . .! Alfie!

Edie, in coat and headscarf, comes rushing on

Edie Alfie . . . Oh, there you are, thank God. What the hell's going on? It's nearly seven.
Alfie We're all right. (*To the baby*) Aren't we, Tommy?
Edie Me and your dad have been worried sick. (*She hits him*) You know you must have him home by half-past five!
Alfie (*protecting himself*) Stop frettin'. He likes fresh air.
Edie And who's this . . .?
Daft Lizzie (*turning to her*) Hallo, Edie. It's me. I'm Lizzie.
Edie Lizzie! I didn't recognize you.

They embrace

How are you, love? I haven't seen you in ages. Are you working?
Daft Lizzie They won't take me on—'cos I'm deaf, see.
Edie They're mad. With all that noise in the mill nobody can hear anyway.
Daft Lizzie He's a bonny baby. I'll bet you love him.
Edie I do, Lizzie. I love him to death. (*She turns the pram to walk home*)
Daft Lizzie I'll bet you're taking him home to his tea.
Edie I am, love.
Alfie Can I stay here, Edie, and play with the other kids?
Edie Do what you like—as long as you're home before dark, mind.
Daft Lizzie (*following Edie*) Can I walk with you?
Edie Course you can.
Daft Lizzie Can I . . . can I push him?
Edie (*touched by her simplicity*) Yes, love, you can push him.

Daft Lizzie takes the handle-bar of the pram, gingerly at first, but then proudly as she pushes the pram off alongside Edie

Alfie (*aside*) So that strange, simple woman turned out in the end,
To be Edie's and Tommy's very best friend.

We might have had nothing, but God, we were happy,
Just us and now Lizzie to change Tommy's nappy.
My job was over, I could play in the park.
But I always promised Edie I'd be home before dark!

Alfie runs off

The Lights change to represent the cotton mill. The almost overpowering sound of the factory rises again as women in wrap-over overalls, turbans and a couple of hair curlers stand at their frames and mime piecing-up. At the same time men and boys in overalls weave in and out of the women, pushing rough wooden trolleys on wheels which contain bobbins: some with crude cotton, some empty. As they work, and above the noise of the machines, they all sing "South of the Border" by Jimmy Kennedy and Michael Carr

Betty and Doris begin to dance together during the second verse

After a few moments, suddenly the sounds of the machines stop dead. Everyone looks about them mystified. The singing fizzles out to silence

1st Worker What's going on?
2nd Worker Why have we stopped?
3rd Worker It's not another bloody war, is it?

Various other mutterings of bewilderment

Alan Tweedale enters looking important. He is a good-looking young man, a cut above the rest in a smart suit and tie. He is followed by Maurice Huggins and Edie

There is lots of muttering

Maurice (*standing on a box*) Could we just have your attention for a minute, please?
Doris Have you run out of shillings for the meter, or what?

Cheers and laughter from the crowd

Joyce (*to Betty*) What's Edie been up to now?
Betty Sticking up for the workers. Nobody else has the guts to.
Maurice (*shouting*) Can we have some hush, please! Now, as you can see, we have Mr Tweedale Junior with us.
Doris God! Summat *must* be up, eh, girls?

Calls of agreement, etc.

Maurice Now, let's not be cheeky, shall we? Show some respect. After all, it's Mr Tweedale who pays our wages.

Murmurs of "What wages?", etc.

Lad I only get fifty shillings a week for doing this lousy job.
Tweedale (*stepping up on to the box*) If I may, I'd just like to have a word, please. We don't want the mill at a standstill for too long, do we? (*He attempts a half-smile*) Now, I'm not sure how many of you are in on this, or indeed how many of you support this young woman here, but Miss Hill has come to me threatening some kind of strike action unless we increase your wages.
Betty (*calling out*) Good old Edie . . .!
Doris (*calling out*) You show 'em, love!
Joyce (*afraid*) Shhh, Betty, Doris. Be careful . . .!

Silence. The rest look over to Betty and Doris

Tweedale Now, my father and I would never want it said that we are anything less than fair. So I'm giving Miss Hill here a minute, and only a minute, to put her case in public. Miss Hill.

Tweedale steps down from the box and gives Edie a hand to step up. Cheers for Edie from the crowd

Edie (*holding up her hands for silence*) Come on now, shut it will you? You heard him—I've only got a minute.

Silence

Right now, you all know what I feel . . . I've worked in this mill since I left Dorothy Street School when I was fourteen . . . and like me dad and me mam—till she died anyway—and the rest of you here, I'll probably be here till I'm sixty. Now, you all know me dad . . . hard working . . . never had a day off in his life . . . frightened to death of losing his job . . . and look at him . . . lungs full of cotton—fighting for his breath half the time. Emphysema our doctor calls it—and there's no cure. Even I, at my age, wake up in the night coughing me lungs up. All right. It can't be helped—it's our job—and where else can we work? But for three pounds a week? Three pounds! I ask you. While up at Cawley and Cunliffe's they're paying three pound ten shillings; and, so I'm told, The Neva in Oldham pay four pound two and six! So, Mr Tweedale, it's not as if we're asking for the moon. We just want you and your dad to recognize our hard work and loyalty by giving us an increase of ten bob a week!

Cheers from the crowd

Tweedale And what if my father and I feel we cannot afford that, Miss Hill? What if I were to explain that in order to keep running costs down and production and out-put high—thus ensuring that this factory stays open and you and your colleagues here remain in work—wages must be kept under control. Wages, I might add, which are totally reasonable and fair for the cotton industry. What then, Miss Hill? Does that make a difference to your demands?
Edie It makes no difference, Mr Tweedale. These are poverty wages and if we can't get what we deserve then by God we'll strike!

Betty and Doris throw up their arms and cry "Yeah!" Joyce is too timid to join them. She turns away

Joyce I think Mr Tweedale has a point.

Various nods of agreement from the crowd. Their mood has obviously been shifted

Edie Come on, the rest of you. We've discussed all this time and time again . . . I need your support.

Silence. Downcast looks

Tweedale You seem only to have two people on your side, Miss Hill.
Betty (*taking hold of Joyce's arm and forcing it up*) Three!

Betty and Doris weave in and out of the crowd trying to gain their support

Tweedale I think you had better step down, Miss Hill.

Edie, almost in tears, tries to step down unaided but falls to the ground. An intake of breath from the crowd brings Betty and Doris rushing to her aid. Edie stays on the floor, seemingly hurt

(*Back on the box*) I do feel it only fair to warn you—all of you—that a strike in this factory would not be tolerated. My father has had a cotton mill in this town since nineteen-eighteen and he's a decent man. He may be firm—some may call him strict—but he's a fine man, a splendid employer and always, always scrupulously fair. Strike and you'll all be out of work with no money at all. I hope that is clear. Now, can we get these frames running, please? (*As he steps down*) I'll see you outside, Huggins!

Maurice Right, Sir. (*To the crowd*) Come on, you lot, back to work. (*Almost hissing to Edie before he goes*) You stupid cow!

Maurice follows Tweedale across L

The sound of the machines starts again as the Lights on the factory start to fade. Edie remains on the floor with Betty and Doris crouched beside her

As the factory Lights fade a Light comes up DL *on Maurice Huggins and Alan Tweedale. The sound of the machines dips slightly to accommodate the following*

Tweedale My father wants that girl out of here, Huggins.

Maurice (*always the crawler*) Yes, Mr Tweedale. But how?

Tweedale You're the gaffer—use your head.

Maurice We could say she's a trouble-maker.

Tweedale No good. We don't want our rivals to think we have "trouble". Everything runs smoothly here at Tweedale's.

Maurice Right, sir. How about . . .?

Tweedale Well?

Maurice Well, she is a bit of a cripple, sir. The work's too dangerous? Might fall into the machinery and hurt herself?

Tweedale Bit of a liability to herself, you mean?

Maurice Always the good of the workers at heart, sir. Sounds good.

Tweedale See to it. And we shall hold you responsible for any further trouble, Huggins, so think on! (*He turns to go off* L)

Maurice (*following him off*) Oh, and might I congratulate you, sir . . . on your engagement to Miss Bracewell!

Maurice and Tweedale exit

The Lights fade up on factory area

Betty (*annoyed*) Scabs, the lot of you!

Doris You couldn't even stand up for us, could you? You miserable lot of gits, you're nothing else!

Betty Yeah—scum, the lot of you!

Edie Leave 'em, Betty. They're afraid of losing their jobs, that's all.

The factory hooter sounds for the end of the day's work. The machines grind to a halt. Edie, with a sigh of relief, makes quickly for the toilet. Betty and Doris, concerned, follow after her as the other girls stop work. They put on coats and scarves, pick up bags, etc.

Joyce, embarrassed, hurries away and exits

Peggy That's it, girls.
Hettie Another day, another dollar!
Joan What're you doing tonight, Eileen?
Eileen Washing me hair—Friday night's Amami night, remember?
Marlene (*to Hilda*) I shall go to the flicks. Why don't you come?
Hilda Can't—got a date.
Joan Which one are you seeing tonight, then? Fred or Harry?
Hettie I've no date.
Marlene Who with, Hilda?
Hilda (*sotto voce*) Harry!

Marlene pulls a knowing face back at her

Eileen Who cares? They're both soddin' useless! Good-night all!

Eileen exits. The remainder, shouting their various "Good-nights" to each other, exit

Peggy Good-night, Betty. Good-night, Doris. (*Embarrassed*) Good-night, Edie.

Peggy exits hurriedly

Only Edie, Betty and Doris are left

Doris I notice that Joyce Tattershall's hopped it quick. Just you wait till I see her on Monday.
Betty (*to Edie*) How're you feeling, love?
Edie Me leg's gone all numb—the good one too.
Betty (*in fun*) Never mind—it'll make a pair.

Maurice Huggins enters from L. *He carries a large brown envelope*

Maurice (*calling*) Hey! You! Edie Hill. I want a word. In private, please.
Betty Anything you've got to say to her, Maurice Huggins, can be said in front of us—right, girls?

Doris Yes. We're comrades, we are.

Maurice Oh, yes? You'll be voting flippin' Communist next, will you? (*He hands Edie the envelope*)

Edie What's this?

Maurice What d'you reckon? Your cards. You're fired!

Betty She's what?

Maurice You heard. I want her off these premises in (*he looks at his watch*) . . . five minutes!

Doris What's the reason? Just because she had the guts to stand up for herself and the rest of us?

Maurice She's a cripple. A liability. It wouldn't be humane to keep her on.

Betty You're a heartless swine, Huggins. I hope your balls drop off tonight!

Doris Yes, while he's playing with himself in the bath. 'Cos no woman would touch you with a ten-foot barge pole!

Maurice (*smug*) Oh no? (*He smiles, looking at Edie*) I don't do so bad for meself.

Full of himself, Maurice exits L

Betty (*suspicious*) What did he mean by that, Edie?

Edie (*covering up*) Take no notice. He's always braggin', he is.

Doris (*putting her arm round Edie*) Oh, Edie—we are sorry, love. Aren't we, Betty?

Betty How will you manage, love?

Edie I'll manage. I have before—I will again!

Music as the Lights fade

Spot on Alfie DR (*to cover change*)

Alfie Dad had often warned Edie about being quiet,
"Just get on with your work and don't start a riot!".
But would she be told? No, she opened her gob,
And now, as you've seen, she's just lost her job.
But that wasn't the worst thing to happen that day,
I ran into Eric who had this to say . . .

Eric enters running

Eric (*distressed*) Alfie, Alfie—have you heard?

Alfie What?

Eric I say have you heard?

Alfie (*impatient*) Have I heard what, Eric?

Eric It's your dad.

Alfie Me dad! What about him?

Eric He's had a bad do—his chest an' that—they're taking him home—you'd better come quick!

Both lads run off as the Lights come up on Daft Lizzie

The bed is pushed into place as Daft Lizzie wheels the pram on. The Lights come up on Edie's house. Daft Lizzie is rocking the pram and singing softly to the baby

Daft Lizzie (*singing softly*)
Little man, you're crying,
I know why you're blue,
Someone stole your kiddy-car away,
Dry your eyes and sleep now,
I'll watch over you,
Little man you've had a busy day.

Alfie (*off; calling, distressed*) Lizzie—come quick! Me dad's been taken poorly . . .!

Alfie rushes on leading four men who are bearing Dad. Dad is trying desperately to get his breath

Not hearing them, Daft Lizzie continues to sing to the baby

Alfie (*tugging at her*) Lizzie—it's me dad—he's poorly again—shall I go and fetch Irish Mary?

Bearer Where shall we put him, missus?

Daft Lizzie (*in panic*) Another attack is it? Bloody cotton! Put him on the bed, please.

Alfie (*distressed; urgently*) Shall I fetch Irish Mary, Lizzie? She always knows what to do.

Bearer (*the four of them having put Dad on the bed*) He collapsed at work, missus. No word of warning. Bad chest, I reckon.

Daft Lizzie (*not hearing*) Thank you very much. Edie'll be home in a minute. She'll see to him.

Bearer I should fetch the doctor, missus. He looks bad.

Alfie It's no use telling her. She can't hear you.

The Four Bearers exit out to the street

(*At the bed with his Dad*) Dad. Dad. What shall I do?

Dad (*gasping for breath*) Sit me up, lad . . . sit me up . . . I can't lie down when I'm like this.

Alfie signals to Lizzie to come over and help lift Dad. She goes over and they both manage to sit him up on the bed

Dad Where's Edie? I'll wring her blasted neck!

Alfie Why—what's she done now?

Dad What's she done? Makin' a right fool of herself at work—showing off like she always does . . . (*He has a fit of coughing*)

Alfie I'm going for Irish Mary, Lizzie—he's really bad.

Irish Mary enters

Irish Mary Don't worry—I'm here. I saw 'em carrying the daft Protestant bugger home.

Alfie Do something, Irish Mary, please.

Irish Mary (*taking one look at Dad*) Go now and fetch Doctor Hempling —explain things to him——now go! Like the wind, lad . . .!

As Alfie runs out into the street he bumps into Edie, who has heard the news and run on from round the corner

Edie How is he?

Alfie He's ever so bad, Edie. The worst I've ever seen him. I'm going for the doctor.

Edie All right—and hurry!

Alfie rushes off up the street

Edie comes into the house, removing her coat and scarf. Irish Mary is loosening Dad's shirt, etc. Daft Lizzie is trying to get his clogs (boots) off

Daft Lizzie (*seeing Edie*) He's bad again, Edie. What shall we do?

Edie (*cradling Dad in her arms*) Lizzie, get Tommy to bed, love, would you? I don't want him seeing all this. Mrs Mulligan, would you brew him some of that balsam in the kitchen? It always seems to help him.

Irish Mary (*rolling up her sleeves as she goes out to the kitchen*) This is the good Lord punishing the old sod for all his evil Protestant ways . . .

Irish Mary exits. So does Daft Lizzie, pushing the pram off

Edie and Dad are left alone in just a pool of warm Light round the bed

Dad What've you been up to again, our Edie?

Edie They've sacked me, Dad. Those bastards have sacked me!

Dad I can't get me breath . . .

Edie (*hugging him, crying*) I know, love, I know . . . the doctor will soon be here.

Dad You mustn't cause trouble, Edie . . . it doesn't always do to cause bother.

Edie Don't worry about it, Dad. I've always got you, and our Alfie—and Tommy . . .

Dad I can't . . . I can't . . . (*He is gasping for air*)

Edie (*holding him, distressed*) That bloody, bloody mill . . . it's killing us all!

Edie and Dad freeze

A Light comes up DL *and Alfie runs on*

Alfie (*aside*) I ran and I ran and was there in a minute,
The surgery was empty, nobody in it,
The doctor said, "Right, I'll just get me bag",
But when we got back, it was that old Irish hag,
Standing in't street; she told me to wait,
Then turned to the doctor and said, "You're too late".

Irish Mary comes across to Alfie and embraces him

The moment is held only briefly before lots of bright coloured Light fills the stage. Before long the stage is filled with as many of the company as possible all doing the "okey-cokey". Irish Mary, Edie and Dad get swallowed up in the crowd and exit. The bed can also be removed unnoticed

The entire company are now in their Sunday clothes (1947). Doris, Betty and Maurice Huggins, who seems to be with Joyce, are in the crowd. Maurice has already had a skin-full

Company (*singing sotto voce at first to allow Alfie to be heard above them, they perform the actions with the song*)
Oh, okey, okey, cokey!
Oh, okey, okey, cokey,

Oh, okey, okey, cokey,
Knees bend—arms stretch—
Rah, rah, rah!

Alfie crosses in front of the performing company and is joined by Eric Schofield

Alfie (*aside; over the above*)
On Friday nights it was straight down the pub,
A break from a week in that evil sweat tub,
Two pints, five Woodbines, the odd punch with your fist,

Maurice punches a guy and knocks him out

Who cared if everyone ended up pissed?
(*He puts his arm round Eric*)
Eric and me, we were well under age,
But with nose pressed to window, it was just like a stage,
The music, the sing-songs, and dancing as well,
A night up in heaven after a week of pure hell!

Alfie and Eric look on from the sidelines as the company now sing out loud and clear

Company You put your right leg in,
Your right leg out,
Your right leg in,
And you shake it all about,
You do the okey-cokey and you turn around,
That's what it's all about—See!

Oh, okey, okey, cokey,
Oh, okey, okey, cokey,
Oh, okey, okey, cokey,
Knees bend—arms stretch—
Rah, rah, rah!

You put your left leg in,
Your left leg out,
Your left leg in,
And you shake it all about . . .(*etc.*)

Under cover of all this, at the back of the stage, two trestles are laid out with a board across them. Dad (now dead) is laid out on the board and covered with a white sheet. At an appropriate moment the company parts in the middle to reveal the body

The company freezes and stops singing. The Lights on them fade slightly as a much brighter, harsh white Light encircles the tableau: Irish Mary, again looking like a washer-woman, has been laying out and cleaning the body. She stands, sweat on her brow, holding a bowl of steaming water and towels. Edie is looking on, holding the baby

Irish Mary There we are. It's the best I can do for him. I've even cleaned his fingernails. They were disgusting!
Edie He looks lovely, Mrs Mulligan. I can't thank you enough.
Irish Mary Ah, sure, you're welcome. It's the least I can do—even though he was a heathen! God save him!

The Light on them fades as the pub lights return and the singing and dancing continues, covering the tableau again

Maurice Huggins has Joyce pinned up against a wall, trying it on. Joyce, although protesting, is secretly enjoying the attention. Betty and Doris are involved with the song

Eventually the song ends and everyone sits about laughing, talking, drinking, etc. Betty and Doris move to the other side of the stage from Maurice and Joyce. Maurice's hand explores Joyce's nether regions

Joyce Gerroff, Maurice. What sort of girl do you think I am?
Maurice We've established what sort of girl you are, Joyce. We just need somewhere to go.
Joyce (*aware that Doris and Betty have an eye on her*) Now, stop it. What would my mother say?
Maurice I don't fancy your mother, Joyce. It's you I'm after.
Betty (*to Doris*) What's she up to over there?
Doris Who cares? She can get stuffed after what she's done to us today.
Betty By the looks of it she will.

Joyce waves over to them and smiles while Maurice bites into her neck

Betty (*ignoring her*) Have you seen Dracula over there, Doris? And she always acts so innocent.
Doris They're the worst sort. (*She looks over*) A bit of salt and vinegar and there'll be no Joyce left.

Alan Tweedale enters with Lydia Bracewell, his fiancée. They look just a bit too smart for this small back street pub

There is an immediate reaction to their unexpected presence

Betty Oh, my God. Have you seen what the cat just dragged in, Doris?

Doris (*looking over; gobsmacked*) I don't believe it. What in the world is he doing here? And who's she?

Betty Surely you've heard. It's Miss Lydia Bracewell—his fiancée.

The entire company freezes

Alfie (*aside*) Miss Bracewell was posh and ever so pretty,
She lived in a big house just outside the city,
I'd seen her a lot since she taught at our school,
No mill for her, no clogs—she was no fool.
But what in the world were they doing here?,
He was up to no good—that much was clear!

Lydia I feel very awkward, Alan. Couldn't we go somewhere else?

Tweedale Relax, dear. I want this lot on my side.

Maurice (*rushing over*) Mr Tweedale—Miss Bracewell—what a pleasant surprise. What can I get you?

Lydia A lemonade for me, Mr. Huggins.

Tweedale Oh, come along. Lydia—we're celebrating. She'll have a port and lemonade and I'll have a double scotch.

Maurice's face falls a mile—he doesn't have that sort of money. Tweedale obviously knows this and enjoys the joke

Tweedale Don't worry, Huggins. I'll buy these. In fact . . . (*He raises his voice commanding attention*) if I may just have everyone's attention . . .

Glasses are tapped, etc. until the whole pub is silent

Betty (*quietly to Doris*) He's a creep and a half, he is.

Doris What's he up to?

Tweedale I'd like to just announce—for the sake of those who don't know—that Miss Bracewell and I have recently become engaged.

There is no reaction at all

And I said to Lydia this evening, didn't I, dear? . . . What better place to celebrate our good fortune than amongst our friends and employees at *The Staff and Dragon*!

Lydia feels awkward. What is *he talking about?*

Maurice (*a lone voice*) Three cheers for Mr Tweedale and the future Mrs Tweedale! Hip- hip . . .

Silence. Tweedale is not going down well. He has to think quickly

Tweedale A moment, please. We have another matter to celebrate, Mr Huggins. I've spoken with my father this evening . . . as you may know he's a rather sick man these days but, as always, he has the interests of his loyal and hardworking work-force at heart. I put it to him and he heartily agreed . . . that from the end of next month . . . Tweedale's will be paying three pounds five shillings a week to every member of staff who has been with us for two years or more!

This does the trick. There are excited murmurings all round

Edie comes on quietly and stands with Alfie and Eric who are seeing all this through a "window". She has overheard the last remarks

Tweedale And if I may—I'd like you all to celebrate, not only my engagement to Miss Bracewell here, but to the future of Tweedale's Cotton Mill. Landlord—drinks all round, please—on me, of course!

There is chaos—a clamour for the bar. Calls of congratulations and hand-shakes for Tweedale and Lydia

Betty (*to Doris*) The smarmy bugger!

Edie (*obviously badly affected by all this*) Come on, Alfie, it's dark. Time we were home in bed!

Alfie (*enjoying himself*) Oh, Edie, can't I just . . .?

Edie (*sharply*) Alfic—just do as you're told for once and get home. This is no place for the likes of us.

Alfie and Eric start to move off

Alfie Come on, Eric. She's always the same when she's got a mood on her.

Alfie and Eric exit

Edie takes one last look through the "window" then turns to go. Maurice Huggins, who has spotted her at the window, comes rushing out into the street

Maurice (*drunk*) Edie . . . Edie!
Edie What do you want?
Maurice Just to say I'm sorry about your dad.
Edie What do you care?
Maurice (*getting her up against the wall, both his arms preventing her escaping*) Come on, fair's fair, Edie. Not havin' much luck are you?
Edie Get out of my way, Maurice.
Maurice I could get you your job back, you know. Tweedale an' me, we're just like that!
Edie Come off it.
Maurice I'm not kidding, Edie. You'd like your job back, wouldn't you?
Edie You know I would. I need the money. 'Specially now Dad's gone. (*Desperately*) Could you help me, Maurice . . . could you?
Maurice (*suggestively*) It'd cost you—you know that.
Edie (*trying to get under his arms*) I'm not interested! Now let me go.
Maurice I'd be careful, Edie—you know that.
Edie That's what you said last time and look what happened—now sod off!

She kicks him where it hurts and rushes off up the street

Joyce (*jumping up on to a table*) Now then, what about it? (*She lifts her glass*) Three cheers for Mr Tweedale! Hip-hip . . .
All Hooray!
Joyce Hip-hip . . .
All Hooray!
Joyce Hip-hip . . .

The crowd lift the glasses and hats for the last "hooray!" . . . but everything freezes. In the street Maurice is holding his sore bits

Maurice (*calling*) Just you wait, Edie Hill! I'll get my own back—you see if I don't . . .!

The Lights start to fade as one bright pool remains DR

Alfie walks into the pool of Light

Alfie All right, you can go for a drink and a smoke and a talk,
But it's not over yet by a very long chalk!

Black-out

CURTAIN

ACT II

A sunny Sunday morning. Some years later

Members of The Salvation Army enter through the theatre singing "Onward Christian Soldiers"

As they enter, the first pool of Light comes up on stage revealing an unusual sight: Abraham Lincoln, Junior and his mate Buzz, both black American G.I.s in uniform, watch and smile as the band moves towards the stage

Eric Schofield is the one carrying and banging the drum. The rest carry and shake tambourines. They are led by Miss Keegan, who carries a banner which declaims "Knock three times and ask for Jesus!"

Another Light comes up on Alfie. He is older now and wears long trousers. He is leaning on the wall DR *his hands in his pockets*

More Lights come up as people enter to greet the band on stage: Percy and The Mulligan Boys (all in long trousers now), Irish Mary, Daft Lizzie, etc. All stare at Abe and Buzz as if they were creatures from another planet

The Lights are fully up as The Salvation Army form a circle on stage. The sound of distant church bells ring out. It ought to be a glorious sight as people clap to the sounds of the hymn

Sally Army Onward Christian Soldiers,
Marching as to war
With the cross of Jesus
Going on before!

Like a mighty army
Moves the Church of God
Onward into battle . . . (*etc.*)

The hymn ends and the company freezes. Alfie steps forward and addresses the audience

Alfie To me, Sunday mornings were best in our street,
Shining, clean faces, clothes pressed and neat,
The old Sally Army with Eric on the drum,
Telling us loudly that Jesus had come!

Eric (*calling to heaven*) Hallelujah!!!

Animation from the crowd as Miss Keegan, banner aloft, steps into the circle

Miss Keegan (*loud and clear*) May I wish you a good morning, Brothers and Sisters . . . I have a message . . . a glorious message . . . it's a message of good hope . . . and the message is from God Almighty who tells us not to be afraid but to throw up our arms and rejoice! . . . for He has sent His only begotten Son, The Lord Jesus Christ . . . and it's good news, Brothers and Sisters, because He's with us this morning . . .

Eric (*banging his drum*) Hallelujah!!!

Miss Keegan Jesus is here in our midst . . .!

A boy (Tommy), dressed and looking as Alfie did in Act I (and played by your smallest actor), appears from the crowd and looks up in wonder at Abe and Buzz

Tommy (*calling out*) Is this Him? Is this Jesus?

The crowd laughs and freezes again

Alfie (*annoyed, calling*) Tommy! Come here and stop showing us up!

Tommy comes over to Alfie and stands holding his hand

Abe (*addressing the silent, frozen crowd*) Pardon me . . . I'm looking for a certain Miss Dolories De Barr . . . number three, Clark Brow . . .?

Alfie (*aside*) As you can see, the years have rolled by,
This is our Tommy and don't ask me why,
But considering the way he was born and begot,
He's more than contented with his little lot.
Edie adores him, and he worships her, too,
He reads books with no pictures all the way through!
He's good at his sums; he can point out Japan,
And he helps with the housework whenever he can.

Animation as Edie comes on in an overall and carrying a mop and bucket

Edie Tommy, you little bugger, I thought you were mopping my front step for me!

She is suddenly aware of The Salvation Army and claps a hand to her mouth

Miss Keegan Edith Hill, really! Please remember what day it is!

Edie I'm ever so sorry, Miss Keegan—it just slipped out like!

Miss Keegan (*looking to heaven*) I'm sure if we ask, the Good Shepherd will forgive this poor fallen sinner. What do you think, Brothers and Sisters?

Eric (*banging his drum*) Hallelujah!!!

Alfie (*aside*) Poor Eric—that's all he knows!

The members of The Salvation Army shake their tambourines calling. "God is good!", "God forgives all sinners!", etc.

Miss Keegan "And the Lord said, 'Come forth'——"

Percy (*interrupting*) —but he came fifth and won a teapot!

Irish Mary clouts Percy round the ears

Irish Mary You wicked, heathen ejit!

Miss Keegan Jesus is in our midst, Edith Hill, and don't you ever forget it.

Edie Yes, well, I wish He'd come and mop my front door step 'cos our little Tommy won't! (*She signals to Lizzie*) Lizzie, come on . . . I need a hand with the washing, love!

Daft Lizzie, reading her lips, goes across to Edie

Tommy (*running over to Edie*) That's Him, Mam—that's Jesus—over there. (*He points to Abe and Buzz*)

Edie Oh, ay? And who's the other one . . . the Holy Ghost? (*She slaps his backside*) Now get in and put your Sunday pullover on . . . showing me up!

Tommy runs off

Meanwhile The Salvation Army have been handing out small pictures of scenes from the Bible

Edie (*to Irish Mary*) Who are those two anyway?

Irish Mary Search me, Edie. One's King Kong and the other's the very devil himself, I shouldn't wonder. (*She crosses herself, then to* *her sons*) And you lot behave yourselves now, or I'll have the scalps off you!

Irish Mary exits blowing her nose on her sleeve. The Salvation Army break into "What a Friend We Have in Jesus" as they march off across the stage and off. The crowd all follow them off, some singing, some jeering. Alfie runs after them

Edie (*calling to Alfie*) Alfie—I'm warning you—if your dinner's ruined . . .!
Alfie (*calling as he goes*) Don't worry—I'll be back!

The street is now empty except for Edie and Daft Lizzie R *staring at Abe and Buzz,* L, *who in turn stare across at them*

Edie (*hitting Lizzie on the arm*) Stop staring, Lizzie!
Daft Lizzie I'll bet one of 'em's Paul Robeson—I've seen him on the pictures.
Edie (*calling over to them*) The war's over, you know—long since. (*She turns to go*)
Abe Err . . . pardon us, ma'am . . . I wonder . . . could you help me and my buddy here . . .?
Edie I'll try. (*Lowering her voice, using her lips to Daft Lizzie*) Don't get too close, Lizzie.

Daft Lizzie continues to stare at the men

Buzz (*trying to be friendly*) You see, ma'am—we're strangers round these parts.
Edie You can say that again.
Buzz (*not catching this*) Excuse me . . .?

Both men have that instant, easy American charm which Edie immediately warms to

Edie Never mind, love. (*She holds our her hand*) The name's Hill . . . Edith Hill. They call me Edie.
Abe (*shaking her hand*) Abraham Lincoln, Junior. United States Army. At your service. And this here's my best buddy.
Buzz (*shaking her head*) You can call me Buzz, ma'am.
Edie (*puzzled but smiling*) Buzz . . . and Abraham Lincoln?
Abe Junior.
Edie You're not related to . . .? (*She leaves it unsaid*)

Abe (*laughing*) No, ma'am. Different colour. But we owe him a great deal!

Edie How can I help?

Abe Oh, yeah, sure. (*He consults his bit of paper*) We're looking to find . . . Number three, Clark Brow.

Edie (*suspiciously*) Three, Clark Brow? What do you want three, Clark Brow for?

Abe Now, this could well be one hell of a wild goose chase, ma'am—but we once made the aquaintance of two pretty young ladies from these parts.

Buzz And we used to write to them at that address.

Abe Of course, it's been so long—they may well be married by now and moved house.

Edie I'm sorry. You must be mistaken. I've lived at that address all my life—and my parents before me.

Abe (*puzzled, to Buzz*) Gee, I guess we must have . . . (*A thought*) This *is* the little town of Middlewade?

Edie Middlewade—that's right.

Buzz Lancashire County?

Edie I suppose so, yes.

Abe (*showing Edie his slip of paper*) That's it. You see, Miss Dolories De Barr, three, Clark Brow.

Edie (*laughing*) Dolories?

Buzz And her friend is called Gloria Whitehaven.

Edie Dolories De Barr and Gloria Whitehaven—there's nobody round here with names like that! (*Her smile fades; the penny drops*) Oh, my God! Betty and Doris!

Abe (*in the dark*) Pardon me . . .?

Edie Then you must be Abe?

Abe Yes, ma'am. That's correct. Abe short for Abraham, see?

Edie (*gobsmacked*) Well, I go to the foot of our stairs!

Abe You sure do have a quaint way of talking, ma'am. Just like Dolories, eh, Buzz?

Buzz (*obviously intrigued by Daft Lizzie*) Your friend, there—she doesn't say a lot.

Edie Oh, no. That's Lizzie. She never says much. She's deaf.

Buzz Oh, dear . . . I am sorry.

Edie Oh, she's fine. (*To Lizzie*) I'm telling them you're deaf, Lizzie.

Daft Lizzie (*simply, hands to ears*) I'm deaf!

Edie Look, why don't you come back in a couple of days or so—I'll make some enquiries for you. (*Testing them*) These two girls—Dolories and . . .

Buzz Gloria.

Edie Gloria, yes. They obviously mean a lot to you. I mean—you've come all this way to find them.

Abe (*genuine, sincere*) They mean the world to us, Mrs Hill—they really do.

Edie (*touched by their simple sincerity*) Miss. I'm Miss Hill. But it doesn't matter.

Abe Well, we'll call back here in two days' time, if that's OK by you.

Buzz We'd hate to put you out.

Edie Not at all . . . it's no trouble.

Abe (*raising his hat*) Bye, then. Bye, Miss Lizzie.

Buzz (*raising his hat*) Good-day to you, Miss Edie.

Abe and Buzz exit

Edie, in her simple way, has been charmed by the two soldiers. Music as the Lights on the street start to fade

Lizzie exits

During Alfie's next speech, Edie puts down her bucket and mop rag and, in a dim pool of Light, collects a roll of carpet brought to her by Daft Lizzie (who then exits again) and lays it DC. *Then on her hands and knees she begins to mop round the outer area of the carpet. While Alfie is speaking, and almost unnoticed, an elegant sofa or chaise is placed on the carpet by two extras*

A pool of Light comes up DR *as Alfie walks into it*

Alfie (*aside, during the above action*)
In case you've been counting the years in between,
I can tell you there's seven and they've been pretty lean,
With our Tommy to feed and my belly to fill,
At least till I left school and went to the mill,
Edie went charring for folks better off,
Well, at least there was no cotton so it helped with her cough!
She did for a lawyer, and a dentist called Swale,
And as fate would have it—for a Mrs Tweedale!

The Lights come up around Edie scrubbing the floor on her hands and knees. Mrs Tweedale (Lydia Bracewell from Act I) enters with two cups of tea. She is a kind and gentle woman and, of course, Edie's social superior. Alfie's Light fades as he walks away into darkness

Lydia A cup of tea, Edie.

Edie (*wiping her brow*) Oh, thanks, Mrs Tweedale. I'll have it while I'm working.

Lydia You'll do no such thing. And when will you learn to use the long mop instead of all that business on your hands and knees?

Edie You can't beat elbow grease, I don't care what you say.

Lydia Come and sit down, please. You make me feel terrible.

Edie (*rising*) All right. But five minutes, mind. You pay me to work, remember?

Lydia Two and six an hour. I don't call that pay.

Edie It suits me. And you employ me for far more hours than you need. (*She drinks*)

We notice that while Lydia holds her cup in the saucer, Edie puts the saucer on her lap and holds the cup in both hands

Lydia I'd pay you much more but Alan keeps a close eye on my housekeeping, I'm afraid.

Edie Men! They've no idea, have they? (*She drinks*)

Lydia Do you miss working in the mill, Edie?

Edie It's so long now—and I've got quite used to scrubbing floors for a living. And they're not all as kind as you, you know. This is the only place I get tea in a china cup. In fact, it's the only place I get tea full stop!

Lydia You haven't answered my question.

Edie Do I miss the mill? Yes, course I do. It's all I know, really. It's in my blood. Me mam met me dad there . . . their mam and dad met there . . . now Alfie's there. Your husband and his old man have had their money's worth out of us! (*She laughs*)

Lydia What about Tommy?

Edie He's too young yet to know what he wants. I hope he can escape it, but what else can you do in this town?

Lydia I managed to avoid it by becoming a teacher.

Edie Oh, well, you're Miss Clever Clogs, aren't you?

Lydia smiles. There is no way she could take offence at Edie

I'll bet you've missed that since you got married.

Lydia I have. I can't tell you how much I miss it. Stuck here, hours on end, playing the role of the dutiful housewife. But you know Alan . . . "I'm not having a wife of mine going out to work!"

Edie You're lucky, though.

Lydia Am I?

Edie You've got all you want . . . everything you need. A big posh house on Tangle Hill . . . what more could you want?

Lydia Children, perhaps.

Edie (*understanding her yearning*) I know. It must be hard. There's me, not even married and had a baby—and you, not able to have any.

Lydia It's not me, Edie. It's Mr Tweedale. He's so busy working—making money—getting home late. I'm surprised he even notices me.

Edie I see. (*Slightly embarrassed, not wishing to pursue this subject, she sips her tea*)

Lydia At least as a teacher I was surrounded by children—even though they were other people's.

Edie I've always meant to ask you . . . does Mr Tweedale know I work here for you?

Lydia Of course not. But it wouldn't matter who I employed, Edie. He's never here.

Edie Look, I hope you don't think I'm cheeky, Lydia. Can I call you Lydia?

Lydia I've been asking you to for five years.

Edie It's our Tommy. He's ever so good at school. Miss Keegan says he's the brightest pupil she's had in years.

Lydia That's good. You must be proud of him.

Edie I am, except . . . I'm no help to him. I mean, I was no good at school—I knew I'd end up at Tweedale's anyway. Tommy needs help with his homework and there's sums and poems an' stuff like that and I don't even understand it. He needs help outside of school.

Lydia Can I help in any way?

Edie Well, that's what I thought. He could come to you after school—and I could collect him before it got dark—and I'd pay you of course.

Lydia What rubbish.

Edie Well, I thought, at least I could work here for nothing in exchange for . . .

Lydia I will not hear of it. (*She is obviously thrilled by the idea*) Edie, I think you've just saved my life!

The two women smile at each other as the Lights fade on them

The sound of the famous exit wedding music as an army of wedding guests enter (in half light) and set about transforming the stage: the sofa (chaise) is lifted and carried off with the carpet, etc. from the last scene. At the same time a long, long table, (the trestles from Act I?) with a white cloth pinned to it is set up c. *Each guest brings a chair, puts it at the table and sits on it—glass in hand, flowers in buttonholes, etc. A wedding cake is placed at the centre of the table*

Lots of laughter, the tipsy sort heard at wedding receptions, as the Lights come up revealing this scene: Joyce, in wedding dress, has married Maurice Huggins

Maurice (*standing, drunk, giving his speech*) And as the actress said to the bishop . . .

Joyce (*not happy; why, oh why has she done this?*) Just get on with it, Maurice!

Cries of "I should watch it, Maurice", "Are you going to let her order you about like that?", etc. from the guests

Maurice Now, it only remains for me to thank my lovely in-laws for such a superb wedding tea. (*He raises his glass to a sour looking couple at his side*) God bless you, Mr and Mrs Tattershall for that lovely ham, that black pudding, the lettuce and tomatoes . . .

Joyce (*addressing the guests*) Oh, wouldn't he get on your nerves?

Betty Joyce wants to get on with the honeymoon, don't you, love.

Joyce Betty! Not in front of me dad!

Doris By the looks of the bridegroom you'll be lucky if he stays awake!

Gales of raucous laughter. The sour-faced couple remain sour-faced

Maurice (*drinking his pint*) Anyhow, it only remains for me to say . . .

Joyce You've said that once. You're giving me a headache here.

Percy Ay, ay—she's got a headache already, Maurice.

Alfie I should hurry up, Maurice, before she changes her mind, lad!

Maurice Now, . . .

All "It only remains for me to say . . .!

Maurice (*dazed*) I do believe . . . I'm pissed!

Joyce (*standing up, her veil on crooked*) Ladies and Gentlemen, there will now be dancing to Glen Miller and his Orchestra . . . on records of course.

One of the wonderful Glen Miller tunes begins to play as various couples get up to dance. Betty and Doris move DL *to light up woodbines. Joyce comes over to them, not at all comfortable in her wedding attire*

Joyce You are awful, you two. Showing me up in front of me mam and dad!

Betty You've just got married, Joyce.

Doris Your dad's not provided you with steel knickers, has he?

Joyce And look at him.

They look over at Maurice, who seems to have slumped over the table

The perfect husband. He's been drunk since a week last Tuesday.

Betty We did warn you, Joyce. You won't be told.

Joyce And where's Edie? My very best friend and she didn't even bother to turn up.

Doris She must have her reasons, Joyce. You know Edie—she wouldn't upset you for the world.

Percy Tully and Alfie come over

Percy Excuse me, Betty, how about a dance then?

Betty You're a bit young for me, Percy.

Percy You're too bloody old for me, Betty, but who cares? I fancy a dance, not half an hour in bed.

Doris Just listen to it!

Percy Come on, take a chance! You might like it.

Betty dances off with Percy

Doris You want to watch him, Betty, he's very——

Joyce That's enough, Doris! This is my wedding, remember. I want no dirty talk!

Alfie Can I have this dance, please, Doris?

Doris Course you can, love.

They go off to dance. Most people are dancing. Two of the Mulligan boys—one with Irish Mary, who looks as if she's had a wash—the other with Daft Lizzie, who of course can't hear the music and looks confused

The music changes to "Love Is the Sweetest Thing". Everyone sings as they dance. Lights can be lowered and a mirror ball used to create a lovely slushy atmosphere. Only Joyce is sitting alone and unhappy. Maurice is picking an argument with someone

During the singing and dancing Edie sneaks in DR*. She hisses over to Betty, trying to attract her attention. Joyce, perhaps talking to someone, doesn't notice her yet*

Edie Betty . . . Betty, come here—quick.

Betty (*dancing with Percy*) What is it?

Edie Get Doris—I want you now.

Betty (*to Percy*) Sorry, Percy, I've got to have a word with Edie. (*She grabs Doris from Alfie*)

Both Betty and Doris go over to Edie. The music dips slightly to accommodate the next scene

Betty What's to do?

Doris Is there a fire or what?

Edie Now, just listen, and don't ask any questions, right? Go to our back yard, both of you.

Betty Your back yard? Whatever for?

Edie I said don't ask questions, didn't I? There's nobody at home, our Tommy's up at Lydia Tweedale's so you'll be all right.

Doris What're you up to, Edie Hill?

Edie You'll see, It's a surprise. In fact it's a bloody big surprise—so get gone!

Betty If this is some sort of joke, I'll kill you, Edie!

Doris and Betty, excited but nervous, rush off DR

Joyce (*thrilled, seeing Edie*) Edie . . . oh, Edie—you've come! (*Crying, she rushes over to greet Edie*)

Edie (*embracing her*) Oh, Joyce, you look lovely.

Joyce I don't. I look a bloody mess! I'm really upset, Edie.

Edie (*sitting her down and crouching beside her*) What is it, love? You mustn't cry—it's your wedding day, Joyce.

Joyce Oh, don't leave me, Edie. I'm ever so frightened.

Edie Why, love? What're you frightened of?

Joyce (*keeping her voice down*) Tonight. I'm frightened of tonight. What do I have to do, Edie?

Edie (*sighing*) With Maurice, love, not much. He'll do it all.

Joyce You talk as if you had first hand experience of him.

Edie Listen, Joyce, let me put it this way . . . what's your favourite pudding?

Joyce Apple pie and ice cream. Why?

Edie Well, all you have to do, love, is—when you get to bed and he

. . . you know! Just close your eyes—screw 'em up tight—and think of apple pie and ice cream . . . bloody great plates full of it—right?

Joyce Will that do the trick?

Edie It'll be a lot more exciting than anything that bugger has to offer. Oh, Joyce. Why did you do it?

Joyce I'm getting on, Edie, I don't want to be left on the shelf, do I?

Edie The shelf is very nice, Joyce. I've been on it all me life. It's lovely on the shelf.

Joyce Yes, but somebody gave you Tommy. At least you've got him. I'd have nobody. (*She cries on to Edie's shoulder*)

Edie (*comforting her*) I know, love . . . I know.

The music stops. The company freezes. Lights on the wedding scene snap out as Lights snap on at the front of the stage

Abe and Buzz enter DL *of forestage as Betty and Doris enter from* R

Betty (*as she enters*) If Edie's having us on—I'll wring her neck!

Doris (*entering*) I can't imagine what she means—a surprise!

The two couples freeze as they look across at each other. We can almost hear all four heartbeats; in fact, a heartbeat effect might work well. The sight we behold must be simple and very moving, at first nobody can speak. They look across

Betty (*unable to believe her eyes*) Abe? Is it Abe?

Abe (*simply*) Hi, there, honey.

Doris Buzz? Surely it's not Buzz?

Buzz Hi, sugar. We said we'd come back.

They rush across to each other, meeting C. *Each couple embraces in the warmest possible way*

The music returns and the romantic Lights come back. The mirror ball revolves once more. The couples all start to dance again as Betty and Abe, Doris and Buzz, dancing themselves now, blend into the crowd at the wedding

If possible, one single voice takes up the words of the song

At the appropriate moment, Black-out and silence

As quietly and speedily as possible the company exit taking the table, the cake, the chairs, etc. One chair is placed DR *on which Tommy sits*

with a book in his hands. Behind him stands Lydia, who is listening to him read aloud from Sweet Thursday *by John Steinbeck*

A pool of Light comes up on Tommy and Lydia

Lydia That is splendid, Tommy. You really do read awfully well.
Tommy I don't know what it means, miss.
Lydia Even more remarkable, Tommy. And how could you understand it? Mr John Steinbeck doesn't write for children of your age.
Tommy (*looking at the cover*) *Sweet Thursday*. It's a nice title.
Lydia I have a small surprise for you. Next week, with your mother's permission of course, I shall take you to the Repertory Theatre in Manchester. Would you like that?
Tommy I've never been to a theatre, miss.
Lydia And that is why I'm taking you. We shall go to an early performance. The play is a simple one—with a very good story—so you should have no difficulty in following the plot.
Tommy Is it like the pictures, miss? I often go to the pictures with my mam.
Lydia It's very similar to the cinema I suppose. Except the actors are real and much more exciting.

Alan Tweedale enters

The easy atmosphere immediately changes; both Tommy and Lydia feel ill at ease

Tweedale Who the hell's this?
Lydia Would you mind, Tommy? I think that's enough for today.
Tommy (*rising*) Yes, miss.
Lydia (*awkwardly, for Alan's sake*) Mrs Tweedale.
Tommy Yes, Mrs Tweedale.
Lydia Straight home now. I don't want your mother worried.
Tommy Bye, Mrs Tweedale.

Tommy exits

Tweedale Well, at least he's polite—but who is he?
Lydia Tommy Hill. His mother used to work at the factory.
Tweedale You mean the lame woman? But that child's illegitimate!
Lydia So? He's very bright. I'm helping him out with his school work.
Tweedale Why?

Lydia What do you mean—why? Because I want to. Where's the harm?

Tweedale Oh, well—it's your business. If you want to fill the house with backward boys the school can't handle.

Lydia He is not backward. Far from it. He has the most remarkable capacity for learning. It's nice to be able to help him.

Tweedale What for? What's the point? He'll only end up working for us anyway. You don't even have to pass an eleven-plus to do that!

Lydia He's a very hard worker. He needs to be encouraged.

Tweedale His mother was a hard worker as I remember. We could do with her sort at the mill now. The present lot are bone-idle, man-mad, and full of lip.

Lydia I'm sure if you offered her a job she'd take it like a shot.

Tweedale Do you think so? Ah, but she was a bit of a troublemaker as I recall. Had to fire her.

Lydia Yes, Alan, *and* made it almost impossible for her to get a job in any other mill.

Tweedale You seem to know a hell of a lot about this woman.

Lydia Couldn't you take her on again, Alan? For my sake—please. She'd be eternally grateful.

Tweedale (*sitting, opening his newspaper*) What's for dinner? Not chicken again, I hope. Much more and I'll be laying eggs myself!

Lydia (*about to leave*) Oh, by the way—I shall be going to the theatre next week. I haven't been in ages.

Tweedale (*engrossed in his paper*) Hmmm?

Lydia Never mind—it doesn't matter.

She exits as the Light fades on the scene. He exits in the darkness

The Lights come up on a low brick wall, sitting on which are Betty and Abe, Doris and Buzz. They are looking relaxed and casual in the bright sunshine. All four laugh as the Lights come up

Betty Give over, Abe!

Abe I'm only kissing your neck, for heaven's sake!

Betty People might see.

Doris (*to Buzz*) You're as bad as him. This is not the proper place for all that.

Buzz Where *is* the proper place, Gloria?

Betty (*feeling awkward*) Look, Abe—Gloria and me—we have something to tell you.

Abe Oh, yeah . . . here it comes, Buzz my old buddy.

Buzz (*taking his arm from around Doris' shoulder*) Don't tell us—we've been expecting it. You want us to get lost, right?

Betty No. No, it's nothing like that. Is that what you thought, Abe?

Abe I must admit, it had crossed my mind that you two might find all this a bit too hot to handle.

Betty Rubbish. We don't care what anyone round here thinks, do we, Doris? (*She is aware at once that she's blown it*)

Buzz (*puzzled*) Doris? Who's Doris, for God's sake?

Doris That's what we wanted to tell you, Buzz. I'm not called Gloria at all.

Buzz (*as if he might not even like the name*) You're called Doris . . .?

Doris (*apprehensive*) Yes.

Doris (*to Abe*) And I'm not called Dolories, Abe. My name's Betty.

Abe Betty? Betty De Barr?

Betty No, Betty Bowkley—and she's Doris Fitton. You hate us, don't you?

Abe (*putting an arm round her, relieved the news isn't worse*) Of course we don't hate you. Buzz, do we hate these gorgeous girls?

Buzz (*to Doris*) So you're not Gloria Whitehaven?

Doris No. I made it up. Have you gone off me?

Buzz How in the world can I go off you? Why, my very favourite movie star is Doris Day!

Abe And I have a secret passion for Betty Grable—so what?

Betty Are you really called Abraham Lincoln, Junior?

Abe I sure am, honey. No kidding. Imagine having to go through life with a name like that!

Betty So I'll be Mrs Abraham Lincoln Junior?

Abe I sure hope so . . . Betty.

Doris But, listen . . . how can we marry you? You live over there and we live over here.

Buzz We have it all figured—it's done all the time. We marry you over here, go back over there, and eventually we can have you come over.

Doris (*her face falls*) Eventually?

Betty We'll be G.I. brides, Doris. Like Elsie Taylor and Jessie Cosgrove.

Abe You would like to live in the States, I hope?

Betty I can't wait—can you, Doris? Do you know Alan Ladd and Ronald Coleman and Clark Gable and . . .

Abe Hang on—not so fast—Buzz and I don't live anywhere near Hollywood.

Doris Oh, well, we're not coming then, are we, Betty?

Betty No, we might as well stop here, Doris.

Abe and Buzz look at each other and wink. They get down from the wall

Abe That's it, Buzz.
Buzz Sure is, Abe. (*They walk away, arms around each others shoulders—buddies*)

The girls jump down

Betty
Doris } (*together; calling out*) Here—wait for us . . .!

All four—the guys linking the girls—walk away laughing. The simplicity of the scene should be both funny and touching

The roar of the cotton mill rises as the workers go about their jobs: Alfie, Eric, The Mulligan Boys, Percy plus extras. Maurice Huggins, looking the worse for wear, is there with his clipboard. All the men and women sing "Red Sails in the Sunset" as they work

After a couple of verses Alan Tweedale enters the factory in a flaming temper

Tweedale (*shouting above the din*) Huggins! Huggins!

Alfie tugs at Maurice's sleeve to tell him he's wanted

(*Mouthing the words clearly*) Huggins—I want you in my office—now!

He exits upstage

Various cat calls to and about Maurice as the singing continues

Maurice, looking concerned, exits upstage after Tweedale

A desk and chair have been placed DR, *where Lights now come up*

Alan enters from downstage. He sits at the desk as Maurice enters

The noise and the singing subside to accommodate the following scene

Maurice Anything wrong, Mr Tweedale?
Tweedale Anything wrong, Huggins? You know flaming well what's wrong. You're wrong, Huggins.
Maurice (*playing the innocent*) Why? What've I done?
Tweedale According to that clocking-in machine you've been in late six times in the past fortnight. More often than not you're drunk most afternoons after dinner—and now I've got last month's

figures and production out there is five per cent down, Huggins! That's what's wrong, lad!

Maurice It's not my fault, Mr Tweedale. You're taking on such lazy workers. The real workers have left and gone up to Cawley and Cunliffe's.

Tweedale If anybody so much as mentions Cawley and Cunliffe's to me again I'll hit that flaming roof. I pay you, Huggins, to keep that factory moving.

Maurice And that's what I bloody well do, Tweedale!

Tweedale Look, don't get saucy with me, Maurice. I'll have you outside on the street before you know what's hit you! I can replace you any day of the week.

Maurice I'm a married man now—I've a wife to keep at home.

Tweedale Yes, and that's a pity. Joyce Tattershall was far more hard working than you've ever been. I suppose we'll be losing Betty Bowkley and Doris Fitton next—they're getting married, I hear.

Maurice Look, Mr Tweedale—I'm sorry. It's married life—I can't get used to the different routine, like.

Tweedale I'm sick and tired of your excuses, Huggins. I've given you fair warning. I'm supposed to make me own living out of this lot, you know.

Maurice Give over—you've enough stashed away to open ten factories!

Tweedale Don't get personal, lad . . .

Maurice (*his temper finally gone*) I've had enough of being treated like a door mat.

Tweedale I've told you, I can always replace you—door mats are ten a penny out there.

Maurice I'll bet you there isn't a man out there on that factory floor who'd stick my lousy job for five minutes.

Tweedale (*threatening*) No. But there might be a woman!

Maurice A woman! Out there? You've got to be joking.

Tweedale Not out there, Huggins. But I know somebody who's looking for a job.

Maurice (*turning to go*) Oh, stuff your poxy job up your arse!

Tweedale You're fired, Huggins. Get your cards on the way out!

Maurice (*slamming the door*) Bollocks!

Tweedale (*calling, in a worse temper than ever*) Rita!

Rita, a secretary in high heels, comes running in from upstage

Rita (*terrified of him*) Yes, Mr Tweedale?

Tweedale I want you to bring the old wage files to me, now!
Rita (*turning to go*) Yes, Mr Tweedale.
Tweedale And, Rita . . .
Rita Yes, Mr Tweedale?
Tweedale I shall want a letter typing this afternoon.
Rita OK, Mr Tweedale.
Tweedale And another thing: I want Huggins' cards made up, ready for him to collect in half an hour.
Rita (*amazed*) Have you sacked him, Mr Tweedale?
Tweedale No, Rita—I'm sending him on a holiday to Blackpool.
Rita Oh, that'll be nice.
Tweedale Get out, Rita, please!
Rita Yes, Mr Tweedale.

She exits in the direction she came from

A knock at the downstage door

Tweedale Come in.

Alfie enters with Eric Schofield who is in a very bad way: he can't get his breath

Tweedale What do you want?
Alfie It's me friend, Mr Tweedale—he's very badly. Can't get his breath.
Tweedale What am I supposed to do? Take him to the Nurse.
Alfie She's not there—I think it's her day at Cawley and Cunliffe's.
Tweedale (*seeing Eric struggling for his breath*) He looks bad.
Alfie (*holding Eric by the shoulders*) He is. I've never seen him as bad as this.
Tweedale A cold, I expect. Well, I suppose you'll have to send him home. But I can't pay him if he isn't working. Here, hang on—aren't you Edie Hill's brother?
Alfie That's right, sir.
Tweedale (*calling*) Rita . . .?

Rita comes running in carrying a file

Rita I've found the file, Mr Tweedale.
Tweedale (*quieter now, looking at Alfie*) It's all right, Rita . . . I don't want it.

The roar of the machines rises. The workers are busy, the lads pushing their trolleys

The Lights increase on the factory as the Lights on Tweedale's office fade (strike desk and chair). The workers sing from "The White Cliffs of Dover"

Betty and Doris run in, excited. They are dressed in their overalls and turbans

Betty (*shouting above the din*) Hey . . . listen . . . shut up a minute and listen.

Various cries of "quiet" as the singing stops

(*Above the noise of the frames*) Hey—you'll never guess . . . Edie's coming back!

Various excited calls to one another: "Edie's coming back!", "Edie Hill—she's coming back!", etc.

Doris (*just as thrilled as everyone else*) It's true. Maurice Huggins has got the push—and Edie's coming back!

Resounding cheers. People dance around the mill.

Betty (*shouting*) And she's going to be the overseer! The supervisor!

Workers (*singing and dancing*)
She'll be coming round the mountains,
When she comes—
She'll be coming round the mountains,
When she comes . . . (*etc.*)

Freeze. The Lights fade. The machines stop dead

Through the centre comes Edie in a hurry. She meets Lydia in a pool of Light DC

Edie (*taking both Lydia's hands in hers*) Oh, thank you, Lydia—thank you so much—I know I've got you to thank.

Lydia Nonsense. I think I must have caught Alan on a good day. Congratulations, Edie. No more scrubbing floors, dear. (*She kisses her on the cheek*)

Edie And *me*—an overseer, Lydia. On five pound a week!

Lydia Knowing my husband, he'll make you work for it, Edie.

Edie Who cares? I've always had to work hard. Oh, by the way—our Tommy loved the theatre—he never stops talking about it.

Lydia Good. You won't mind if I take him again? I thought *A Midsummer Night's Dream* this time.

Edie My God! A supervisor—five pound a week—and bloomin' Shakespeare—we're going up in the world!
Lydia (*fondly, sincerely*) And you deserve it, Edie.

Music

The company exits and all the Lights fade. A single pool of Light comes up DL. *Alfie walks into the pool of Light*

Alfie (*aside*) Would you believe it? a bit of good luck!
Edie promoted, our Tommy seeing Puck.
They say that eventually things must go right,
A small, lighted candle in everyone's night.

Sadly, however, it was my turn to go,
But at least I was given a last chance to show
That when He calls your name and says, "It's the end!",
How better to die than to die for your friend?
(*He calls desperately*) Eric . . .! Eric . . .!

Reflected water fills the stage. Dim Lights show the canal bank, some steps and a walk-way high up. Lights from torches roam the semi-darkness

Percy and The Mulligan Boys come from different directions, flashing their torches and calling Eric's name loudly

Alfie (*running up to join the others*) Have you found him, Percy?
Percy There's not a sign of him anywhere, Alfie.
Alfie The times I've told him to stay away from this bloody canal. (*He shouts*) Eric!
The Others (*calling*) Eric!

The word "Eric" seems to echo around the theatre

Johnny When did you know he was missing?
Alfie When I called for him. His mam said he hadn't come home.
Sean Perhaps he has a Sally Army meeting.
Mick Or the St John's Ambulance—he goes there once a week.
Alfie It's Monday—he never goes anywhere on a Monday. (*He calls*) Eric! Can you hear me?

The words echo around

Johnny Should we go to the police station, Alfie?

Alfie Could you? Tell 'em Eric Schofield's missing and he hasn't got his tablets or his inhaler.
Sean Come on, Johnny, Mick—we'll go.

The three Mulligan Boys rush off together

Alfie (*distressed, crying*) Bloody hell . . . Eric!

Distantly, very distantly, there is a cry from Eric

Eric (*off; distant*) Alfie . . . Alfie . . .?
Percy Hey—listen.
Alfie What? What is it?
Percy Shhh! I thought I heard him . . .
Eric (*off; distant*) Alfie . . . I'm over here . . .
Alfie I told you. He's in the canal, Percy. (*He starts to remove his jacket and shirt furiously*)
Percy Hey, what're you doing, you silly bugger?
Alfie I've got to go in, Percy—I've got to save him. (*He strips off his shoes and socks*)
Percy It's pitch black down there—you'll never find him, Alfie. And I didn't know you could swim.
Alfie I can't, but who gives a bugger . . .?

Alfie jumps over the back of the catwalk and down out of sight

The sound of Alfie calling "Eric, I'm here" fills the theatre. The words become elongated like someone falling into a bottomless pit

Percy (*distressed, a cry from the heart*) Alfie!

Silence. The Light slowly fades on Percy, on his knees, weeping, sobbing

Black-out

Percy exits

The Lights come back on the same arrangement of steps and catwalk, etc. We realize at once we are now at a busy railway station. The sounds of a station fill the air: the hissing of steam engines, tannoy announcements, etc. The same mist that might have been used for the canal bank can here become the steam from engines. The catwalk (earlier the canal bank) now acts as number three platform

Extras enter, saying goodbye to loved ones

Betty and Abe, Doris and Buzz enter with Edie. The boys carry suitcases etc.

Edie Oh, Betty . . . Doris—I'm going to miss you!

A tannoy announcement states, "The train now standing at platform three is the half-past eight for Glasgow and Edinburgh. Will all passengers kindly board the train now."

Betty Stop crying, you silly thing. You'll have us at it next. (*She gets a hanky from her bag*)
Doris We'll be back in a fortnight.
Edie But all that way, Doris! What if I never see you again?
Abe Edie—we're only going to Scotland to get married. The girls aren't leaving for the States yet!
Edie But Scotland—it's *miles* away!
Buzz It's the only place they'll marry us, Miss Edie.
Edie (*to Betty*) What shall I tell your mam and dad?
Abe We've got to get aboard, girls. (*He kisses Edie*) Bye, Edie—and thanks for all you've done for us! (*To Betty and Doris*) We'll take the cases, Betty.

Abe and Buzz collect the suitcases and rush off to board the train. A loud hiss of steam from beneath the platform

Edie Well, what am I supposed to tell your parents?
Betty Just say you haven't seen us. Tell 'em we've gone missing or summat.
Doris (*kissing Edie*) Don't worry about it, love.
Edie But what happens when you get back?
Betty (*kissing Edie*) It'll be too bloody late then. We'll be married, Edie!

Joyce comes on running. We notice she is trying to hide a black eye with her hat

Joyce (*rushing on*) Betty—Doris—don't go yet!
Doris It's Joyce—she's come to wave us off.

Sounds of the train starting up. A whistle blows

Betty (*crying; overcome*) Oh, Joyce, love—thanks for coming. (*She embraces Joyce*)
Doris (*also embracing Joyce*) Bye, Joyce—we'll see you when we get back, love.

Abe (*off*) Come on, you guys—you'll miss the train . . .!

Betty and Doris rush off in the direction of the boys, both shouting their goodbyes

Edie and Joyce wave to them frantically as we hear the train moving off. There is lots of hissing steam and a train whistle

The Extras also wave their goodbyes and slowly leave the station, leaving Edie and Joyce alone there

Joyce is really upset

Edie (*her arm around Joyce*) Come on, love—it's not that bad. They'll be back.
Joyce (*sitting on a skip*) At least they're happy, Edie.
Edie (*sitting beside her*) What's the matter, Joyce? (*Seeing her eye*) Hey, what's all this?
Joyce (*trying to hide it*) I'm all right—leave me alone.
Edie Has that bugger been hitting you again? Just wait till I get my hands on him!
Joyce (*terrified*) Don't say anything, Edie. It only makes him worse if he thinks I've been squealing.
Edie You can't go on like this, Joyce.
Joyce (*weeping*) He says I'm useless—he says he'd be better off with half a dozen sheep!
Edie (*almost to herself*) Isn't he the bloody limit!
Joyce And he keeps hinting, Edie.
Edie (*wary now*) Hinting? Hinting about what, Joyce?

In the background Percy, Daft Lizzie and The Mulligan Boys enter, obviously looking for Edie

Joyce I'm not sure. But he keeps mentioning your Tommy.
Edie (*to herself*) The bastard!
Joyce And he'll never forgive you for taking his job.
Edie I didn't take it, Joyce—honest I didn't. Tweedale came to our house and offered me that job.
Daft Lizzie (*coming across to them*) Edie . . . Edie!
Edie Lizzie . . . what are you doing here?

She turns and sees Percy and The Mulligan Boys, caps in hands and looking downcast and fearful

Percy? Johnny—Sean . . . and Mick? (*She knows something is wrong now*) What is it, Percy?

Percy It's bad news, Edie—I'm very sorry.

Daft Lizzie (*crying*) It's Alfie, Edie . . . it's Alfie.

The sounds of whistles, steam, and another train departing swamp the words Percy is saying to Edie

Edie looks stunned as Joyce and Daft Lizzie escort her away

The Lights begin to fade

Loudly, Gracie Fields sings "Wish Me Luck As You Wave Me Goodbye" in the darkness

A Light, brighter than ever, comes up on Alfie. He's still cheerful, still smiling

Alfie (*aside*) Don't sit there crying, there's no point in that
There's nowt new in this story, it's very old hat.
It happened to thousands, not just two or three,
What makes this important is it happened to me!
And you mustn't think Edie's now all on her own,
She's got Tommy and Lizzie and OK, I can't phone,
But I'm up here watching, and I'll do all I can
To see everything down there goes according to plan.

The Lights come up around Tommy sitting on a bench on Tangle Hill. He is reading

We'll move on a bit now—perhaps ten years or more,
And Tommy's expecting his results through the door.
With Lydia's help he should have done well—
But the waiting, as always, is simply pure hell . . .

Alfie remains watching as Tommy, now in a suit and looking older, sits reading his book in the sunshine

After a moment Eric, looking older and frailer, comes up quietly behind him and looks out at the view from the hill

Eric (*breathing heavily*) It's a grand view, lad.

Tommy (*looking up from his book*) Oh, hallo, Uncle Eric. (*Looking out*) Yes, it's a grand view all right. I often come up here if I want time on my own.

Eric (*quietly sitting beside him*) Not studying today?

Tommy No. Nothing to study yet. I've sat all my exams. Just waiting to hear how I've done.

Eric Nervous?

Tommy A bit. You never know, do you?

Eric You'll be fine. You never thought you'd make Grammar School, but you did.

Tommy Yes. (*Always modest*) I've been lucky.

Silence. Both men look across at the view

How's your chest?

Eric Just the same. It won't get any better now, I reckon.

Tommy At least you're out of that factory.

Eric Ay. (*Pause*) Ay, I never went back after . . . after . . . I never went back.

Tommy (*quietly*) No. (*Pause*) Do you ever feel that . . . you're on your own, Uncle Eric? I don't mean lonely—I'm not lonely—just that feeling of being on your own, like.

Eric Ay. Well, I suppose we are really, lad. Mind you—I'm sure we all have somebody watching over us.

Tommy Do you think so?

Eric Oh, I'm sure of it.

Silence. Eric brings a small leather-bound book from his pocket

Eric I've got something for you . . . it's not much—but I'd like you to have it.

Tommy (*taking the book*) What is it?

Eric A little book of poems. It was a school prize. For never being absent and never being late.

Tommy (*moved by this simple gesture*) Are you sure? It must mean a lot to you.

Eric There's an inscription inside.

Tommy (*opening the book and reading*) "To Alfred Hill: Best wishes from the Headmaster and Staff, Dorothy Street Secondary School, Spring nineteen forty-eight."

Eric Alfie gave it to me when I joined the Salvation Army. He said he didn't understand poetry.

Pause

It seemed only right you should have it.

The sound of birdsong at a distance as the two men just stare out into space

Tommy (*softly*) Thank you . . .

Alfie walks from his Light into theirs and stands quietly behind them

Alfie (*aside*) Perhaps on the next day, or the day after that,
The awaited brown envelope appeared on the mat,
Tommy, all shaking, opened it fast,
And the neatly typed message told him—he'd passed!

Excitement as Tommy produces the letter from his inside pocket

Lights come up on the Tweedale house where Lydia, in a dress which makes her look older, is sitting, waiting, Tommy runs across to her as the Lights on Eric and Alfie and the bench fade. Alfie and Eric exit unnoticed

Tommy (*excited*) It's come, Lydia . . . the letter's come. I've been accepted!

Joyce (*just as thrilled*) Oh, Tommy—I couldn't be more delighted.

Tommy I start in September. (*Sitting beside her*) Wow! I still can't believe it.

Lydia Why ever not? You've worked hard enough for it.

Tommy I just didn't think it possible. I always thought you had to have money to go to University.

Lydia Rubbish. You need a brain and the good sense to use it. I did it—why shouldn't you?

Tommy I'm just so excited, Lydia—I can't tell you. (*He jumps in the air and gives a shout of joy*)

Lydia What does Edie say? She must be over the moon.

Tommy (*slightly deflated now*) I haven't told her.

Lydia You haven't . . . why on earth not? She'll be thrilled, Tommy.

Tommy (*sitting again*) Will she? Will she really?

Lydia Don't be silly! Of course she will.

Tommy Oh, she'll say she is. But will she be? It means I have to leave home, Lydia.

Lydia And you'll miss it, I suppose.

Tommy (*quietly now*) Yes. I will, Lydia. I'll miss the cosiness . . . the warmth of the kitchen when it's dark . . . eating our tea together . . . listening to the rain at the windows . . . the clock ticking away on the mantelpiece. Mam listening to the wireless . . . me studying . . . Lizzie singing quietly to herself. (*Pause*) And Mam's going to miss me.

Lydia She'd never dream of standing in your way—you know that.

Tommy (*doubts creeping in now*) And what about money? I'm going to need even more. She's done enough for me.

Lydia You'll have to find a job in the holidays. Or apply for a grant. I'll help you put a letter together—Alan can give you a reference. Don't worry about all that now, Tommy. Just enjoy the success.

Tommy Do you think I can do it?

Lydia Of course you can—you've come this far.

Tommy I could get a job at the mill between now and September, couldn't I?

Lydia If you're that desperate—yes, I suppose you could.

It is obvious he is overwhelmed by it all. He looks at Lydia and smiles warmly

Tommy How can I ever thank you, Lydia?

Lydia (*modest as always*) Oh, now. Please.

Tommy You taught me. Introduced me to great literature—the theatre. You always encouraged me when things got tough. I owe it all to you.

Lydia You owe it all to Edie. She brought you up—worked herself stupid to keep you fed and healthy . . . and never forget it: it was Edie who first had the idea to bring you to me.

Slowly, on another part of the stage, a pool of Light comes up on a table and three chairs

Edie is laying a cloth on the table and setting it with knives and forks, etc. She is now looking older, slightly plumper maybe, all done with clothes, shoes, and hair rather than with make-up. (She must be about 38 by now)

And another thing—I was stagnating here before you came. It was Edie who changed my life. So remember—we've her to thank for all this.

Daft Lizzie, also older, brings in two plates of food and sits at the table with Edie

So go home now, Tom. Go home and tell her. She'll be absolutely delighted—I know she will . . .

The Lights fade on Lydia as she walks away into the darkness

Tommy simply walks around the stage, watching Edie and Daft Lizzie eating, as the Light around the table grows brighter. In the distance "Love Is the Sweetest Thing" plays softly. Finally he comes into the room where they are

Tommy (*quietly, fondly*) Hi, Mam. Hi, Lizzie.

Edie Oh, hallo, love—I didn't think——

Tommy It's OK—I shan't want anything to eat.

Daft Lizzie (*to Edie*) Will he want anything to eat, Edie?

Edie (*putting a hand on Daft Lizzie's arm*) No, Lizzie.

Tommy (*sitting at the table*) I've got good news, Mam. They've accepted me at University.

Edie (*her face lights up*) Oh, Tommy—I'm so glad. It's just what you wanted. (*To Lizzie*) He's passed, Lizzie—he's passed!

Daft Lizzie What does it mean?

Tommy You know, don't you, Mam—that I'll have to go away?

Edie (*trying not to show any concern*) Yes, but it won't be for ever . . . will it?

Tommy Of course not. I'll be home in the holidays.

Edie There we are then. (*To Daft Lizzie*) He'll be home in the holidays, Lizzie.

Daft Lizzie Will he be home in the holidays?

Tommy But it means I'll have to work, Mam. I'll have to get a job.

Edie But why?

Tommy I'll have to earn some money.

Edie But your studies—what about your studies?

Tommy I'll have to combine the two—it won't kill me. And, you never know, I may get a grant from the Education Authorities.

Edie What sort of a job will you get?

Tommy With you in the mill. What else is there?

Edie Never. No, Tommy—not that.

Tommy Why?

Edie Because I say so. The place is evil, love. For my sake, eh? Get a job anywhere—in an office—at the Co-op—anywhere. But not at Tweedale's. Promise me.

Tommy All right—I promise.

Edie Anyway, you might not have to find a job. I've got plenty of money put by for you in the Post Office.

Tommy (*trying to protest*) Now, Mam—the last thing I want——

Edie Hold on—hold on—it isn't my money, it's yours. (*She winks at Daft Lizzie*) Isn't it, Lizzie?

Daft Lizzie She's got a couple of hundred for you in the Post Office.

Tommy A couple of hundred pounds! Where from?

Edie Ah, that'd be telling, wouldn't it, Lizzie?

Daft Lizzie That'd be telling wouldn't it, Edie?

Tommy I can't accept money unless I know where it's from, Mam.

Edie Look, I'm sworn to secrecy—I promised I'd never tell you.

Tommy It's Lydia, isn't it? Am I right?

Edie Mind your own business!

Daft Lizzie Mind your own business, eh, Edie?

Tommy All right—but the least I can do tonight is buy 'em all a drink in *The Staff and Dragon.*

Suddenly we are in the pub. All our regulars plus extras are present (not Betty or Doris or Alfie, for obvious reasons)

The table (cloth removed, etc.) becomes a table in the pub—Edie, Daft Lizzie and Tommy remain at it and an extra gives them glasses of beer

There is music, singing to a piano, Lights, lots of laughing, etc. They sing from "Roll Out the Barrel"

Joyce and Maurice are there. Both have had enough to drink. Sadly, Joyce now looks quite common—she smokes and has a glass of gin in her hand

Everyone sings until the appropriate moment: someone helps Irish Mary up on to a chair or table

Irish Mary (*loudly*) Will you all shut your heathen gobs!

Cries from everyone to shut up. The music stops

Joyce (*drunk, fag in hand, overly made-up*) Shut it—you lot—Irish Mary wants to speak!

Irish Mary They've shut up, Joyce Huggins—it's you who's making all the din!

Joyce Oh, I'm sorry. (*She hiccoughs*)

Irish Mary I'd just like to say a few words about this fine young man here . . . Mr Thomas Hill!

Edie He's never called Thomas, Mary—not ever in this world. His name's Tommy!

Irish Mary You had him christened Thomas, surely?

Edie (*with a cheeky grin and slightly guilty*) I never even had him christened. Why? Was I supposed to?

Irish Mary You never had the poor bugger christened . . . why you . . .

All (*joining in with Irish Mary*) "You wicked, heathen, Protestant bugger!"

Lots of laughter

Irish Mary Anyhow—I'd just like to say that it was me who brought that lad into the world—me—Irish Mary!

Edie (*telling the whole pub*) She thought he was dead—she nearly chucked him down the bloody toilet . . . (*To Tommy*) Didn't she, love?

Tommy (*his arm around Edie*) I'm glad she didn't.

Irish Mary Now, I'd just like to say . . . I have given birth to . . . how many?

Johnny
Sean
Mick
Patrick
Billy
Hugh
(*and as many others as possible*) } (*together*) Thirteen!

Irish Mary Was it really that many? Thirteen—and all of 'em boys, God bless my soul, and not one of 'em is a patch on our Tommy here. And now he's off to . . . where is it?

All University!

Irish Mary I hope it's a good Catholic place anyway. And I want you all to raise your drinks—the drinks he bought us, remember—and wish him Godspeed! (*She raises her glass*) To Tommy!

All (*raising glasses*) To Tommy!

Maurice (*drunk of course, out for bother*) Yeah—he's done well for a little bastard, hasn't he?

Silence. An awful moment for everybody

But then you've got to be a right little bastard to get anywhere in this world. Isn't that right, Tommy, old man?

Irish Mary (*getting down from the table*) Why, you, wicked . . . no-good bundle of . . .

Irish Mary's sons grab hold of her to prevent her killing Maurice, with various cries of "Leave him, Mam", "Watch that Irish temper, Mam", etc.

I'll lay him out on that friggin' floor if I get my hands on him.

Edie Leave him, Mary. He's not worth it. Come on, Tommy—we'd best leave. (*She rises*)

Tommy (*making her sit again*) No, Mother. We're stopping where we are.

Maurice (*getting in closer to Tommy*) Oh, what's this, then? Little Tommy's proving he's not a mammy's boy after all, is he?

Tommy Watch it, Maurice—I'm quite capable of laying you out myself! (*He rises, about to take his jacket off*)

Edie (*afraid now*) Tommy! Don't! Leave him, love!

Maurice Come on, now . . . that's no way to speak to your old dad, is it?

Joyce What's he on about?

Edie Watch it, Maurice—I'll rip your bloody tongue out if you say any more!

Irish Mary (*struggling to be free from her sons' grip*) Let me get at him . . . let me get at that git!

Joyce (*coming to Maurice*) I want to know what you meant by that remark, Maurice Huggins!

Maurice (*pushing her aside*) Sod off, Joyce—get lost! (*Addressing the rest of the pub*) None of you knew that—did you? None of you knew that this woman with the limp, the woman who stole my job, the woman who bore my child, none of you knew she used to be a whore!

Tommy (*white with rage, almost jumping over the table*) Right, that's it, Huggins . . .!

Some men grab Tommy, others grab Maurice

Maurice Come on then, marred-arse—what will you do to me—eh? What will you do?

Tommy (*almost spitting out the words*) Unless you take that remark about my mother back, Huggins, I'm . . . I'm . . .

Maurice What, marred-arse? You couldn't knock the skin off a rice pudding.

Edie is being comforted by Daft Lizzie. Both look terrified

Whether you like it or not, sunshine, I'm your father—and

that mother of yours was a tart! Go and tell 'em that at flamin' University!

Joyce (*going to Maurice who is still being held by the men*) You bastard, Maurice. All this time and you never told me. (*She spits at him*)

Irish Mary Be careful, Joyce—he'll let you have it at home, love!

Joyce Don't worry—I'm never going back to this piece of dog-dirt. (*She turns to Edie, tears running down her face*) Why did you never tell me, Edie? Why did you never say?

Edie Joyce—I couldn't, love. How could I? How could I tell you that?

Joyce (*in a rage, in temper, half-drunk*) You pig! (*This is said to Maurice as she lands out at him with her fist and hits him in the mouth*)

The force of the blow knocks Maurice to his knees. Blood runs from his mouth. Joyce goes over to Edie and takes her arm

Joyce Come on, Edie . . . I'm taking you home. I can't bear to think of you being defiled by that piece of rubbish.

Edie You're not cross with me?

Joyce Cross with you? How could I be? Come on, love . . . can I stay with you tonight? I've nowhere else to go.

Edie (*to Tommy*) I'm sorry Tommy. I should have told you. So often I intended to sit down and explain things—but it wasn't my fault—he made me, Tommy, he made me do it.

Tommy is silent, his head bowed

Please believe me. Please.

Tommy is weeping, unable even to look at Edie

Will you come home? Please come home.

Everyone just looks on, helpless and unable to do or say anything

Joyce leads Edie away

The scene freezes. The Lights go to half. A pool of Light comes up C

Alfie walks through the centre of the crowd and into the Light

Softly, at a distance, a pub piano plays "Love Is the Sweetest Thing"

Total stillness, just Alfie addressing the audience

Alfie I did try from up there . . . I did try ever so hard to make things work out . . . but it's not always possible to create a happy ending. Maybe, just maybe, things could have been different—who knows? Tommy eventually went away . . . he never came home again . . . but every month his money used to arrive . . . there to collect at his nearest Post Office . . . until, of course, one day it ran out. Tommy always assumed the money came from Lydia Tweedale . . . but it was Eric who sent it . . . Eric Schofield . . . a small thank you for me saving his life . . . Edie always wrote to Betty and Doris in the States, but she never saw them again . . . She died, on her own, one wet Monday night, aged fifty-four . . . the cotton finally finished her off . . . Lizzie was put away . . . they said she was daft and unable to look after herself . . . Tommy—who knows what he thinks? . . . He works hard as a teacher . . . but he gets that from his mother . . . He never married—how could he? . . . The revelations that night in the pub haunted him for the rest of his life. But I'm sure he thinks about Edie—even though he never mentions her . . . and without fail, whenever dusk falls, he remembers her remark—and always, if it's possible, he's home before dark!

The sound of a back-street pub piano playing "Love Is the Sweetest Thing" rises as all the Lights begin to fade

CURTAIN

FURNITURE AND PROPERTIES LIST

ACT I

On stage: Bed
Bedclothes
Doorframe
Bowl of steaming water for **Betty**
Soiled towels for **Doris**
Bundle wrapped in a towel for **Joyce**
Chair
Box
Coats
Scarves
Handbags
2 trestles
Board
White sheet
Glasses
Pub furniture
Wall

Off stage: Skipping rope (**Doris**)
Old-fashioned pram with baby (**Alfie**)
Large brown envelope (**Maurice**)

Personal: **Edie:** lollipop, airmail letter with photographs
Betty: stick of rock
Eric: thick glasses and thermos flask
Miss Keegan: whistle, wrist-watch
Doris: three cigarettes, lighter
Maurice: clip-board, pencil

ACT II

On stage: Wall
Roll of carpet
Elegant sofa or chaise
Long table or trestles with a white cloth

Wedding cake
Mirror ball
Chairs
Trolleys
Skip
Bench
Table
3 chairs
Pub furniture

Off stage: Drum (**Eric**)
Tambourines (**Sally Army**)
Banner (**Miss Keegan**)
Pictures of Bible scenes (**Sally Army**)
Piece of paper (**Abe**)
Bucket (**Edie**)
Mop rag (**Edie**)
2 cups of tea with saucers (**Lydia**)
Chairs (**Wedding Guests**)
Glasses (**Wedding Guests**)
2 books (**Tommy**)
File (**Rita**)
Torches (**Percy** and **Mulligan boys**)
Suitcases (**Abe** and **Buzz**)
Tablecloth (**Edie**)
Cutlery (**Edie**)
2 plates of food (**Daft Lizzie**)
3 glasses of beer (**Extra**)

Personal: **Doris:** cigarettes, lighter, handbag
Maurice: clipboard, pencil
Betty: handbag
Eric: small leather-bound book
Tommy: letter (in pocket)
Joyce: cigarettes, glass of gin
Maurice: blood sac

LIGHTING PLOT

ACT I

To open: Bring up spot on **Edie**

Cue 1 **Alfie:** "That was her lot!" (Page 1)
Bring up spot on **Doris, Betty** and **Joyce**

Cue 2 **Joyce:** "... it's moving and it's breathing!" (Page 7)
Black-out

Cue 3 Sound of a baby crying (Page 7)
Bring up spot on **Alfie** DL

Cue 4 **Alfie:** "... one leg shorter than t'other ..." (Page 7)
Bring up spot on **Edie** C

Cue 5 **Alfie:** "... she was nobody's fool." (Page 8)
Bring up school playground effect

Cue 6 **Edie:** "... anything you tell 'em." (Page 9)
Fade to spot on **Alfie** DL

Cue 7 **Alfie:** "... with nothing to hide." (Page 10)
Bring up warm spot on bed

Cue 8 **Alfie** walks away (Page 10)
Fade spot on **Alfie**

Cue 9 Music (Page 11)
Bring up school playground effect

Cue 10 The **Children** sit in a semi-circle (Page 14)
Change to school hall effect

Cue 11 **Miss Keegan:** "Multiplication!" (Page 15)
Black-out; when ready, bring up ladies' lavatory effect DR

Cue 12 **Maurice** smiles to himself (Page 19)
Cross-fade to bright sunshine effect

Cue 13 **Alfie** runs off (Page 21)
Cross-fade to cotton mill effect

Cue 14 **Maurice** follows **Tweedale** across L (Page 24)
Cross-fade to DL

Cue 15 **Maurice** and **Tweedale** exit (Page 24)
Cross-fade to factory area

Cue 16 **Edie:** "... I will again!" (Page 26)
Fade to black-out; bring up spot on **Alfie** DR

Cue 17 **Eric** and **Alfie** run off (Page 27)
Bring up **Edie's** *house effect*

Cue 18 **Irish Mary** and **Daft Lizzie** exit (Page 28)
Bring up warm spot around bed

Cue 19 **Edie** and **Dad** freeze (Page 29)
Bring up spot DL

Cue 20 **Irish Mary** embraces **Alfie;** after a moment (Page 29)
Bring up lots of bright coloured light

Cue 21 The company freezes and stops singing (Page 31)
Fade slightly; bring up harsh white light on **Edie** and **Irish Mary**

Cue 22 **Irish Mary:** "God save him!" (Page 31)
Cross-fade to pub effect

Cue 23 **Maurice:** "... you see if I don't ...!" (Page 34)
Slow fade; bring up spot DR

Cue 24 **Alfie:** "... by a very long chalk!" (Page 35)
Black-out

ACT II

To open: Bring up sunny morning effect; after a moment, bring up spot on **Alfie** DR (Page 36)

Cue 25 People enter to greet the band on stage (Page 36)
Bring up more lights

Cue 26 **Abe** and **Buzz** exit (Page 41)
Fade; bring up spot DR

Cue 27 **Alfie:** "... for a Mrs Tweedale!" (Page 41)
Bring up interior effect; fade spot

Cue 28 **Edie** and **Lydia** smile at each other (Page 44)
Fade to half light; when ready, bring up interior effect

Cue 29 **Doris** and **Alfie** dance (Page 45)
Fade lights to romantic effect

Cue 30 **Edie:** "I know, love ... I know." (Page 47)
Snap off romantic lights; snap on lights on forestage

Cue 31 The two couples embrace (Page 47)
Revert to romantic lights; at the appropriate moment, black-out

Cue 32 **Tommy** reads aloud (Page 48)
Bring up spot on **Tommy** *and* **Lydia** DR; *gradually bring up interior effect*

Cue 33 **Lydia** exits (Page 49)
Fade to black-out; when ready, bring up bright sunshine effect

Cue 34 All four walk away laughing (Page 51)
Change to cotton mill effect

Cue 35 **Maurice** exits (Page 51)
Cross-fade to office effect DR

Cue 36 **Tweedale:** "I don't want it." (Page 53)
Cross-fade to cotton mill effect

Cue 37	The company freezes *Fade; bring up spot on* **Lydia** DC	(Page 54)
Cue 38	The company exits *Fade to black-out; bring up spot* DL	(Page 55)
Cue 39	**Alfie:** "Eric ...! Eric ...!" *Change to dim lighting with reflected water effect*	(Page 55)
Cue 40	**Percy** falls to his knees *Slow fade to black-out; when ready, bring up railway station effect*	(Page 56)
Cue 41	**Edie, Joyce** and **Daft Lizzie** exit *Fade slowly to black-out. When ready, bring up very bright spot on* **Alfie**	(Page 59)
Cue 42	**Alfie:** "... according to plan." *Bring up spot on* **Tommy**	(Page 59)
Cue 43	**Alfie:** "... told him — he'd passed!" *Bring up* **Tweedale** *house effect; fade spots on* **Alfie** *and the bench*	(Page 61)
Cue 44	**Lydia:** "... to bring you to me." *Bring up spot on table and chairs*	(Page 62)
Cue 45	**Lydia:** "... I know she will ..." *Fade on* **Lydia;** *increase on* **Edie** *and* **Daft Lizzie**	(Page 62)
Cue 46	**Tommy:** "... in *The Staff and Dragon.*" *Change to pub interior effect*	(Page 64)
Cue 47	**Joyce** leads **Edie** away *Bring down to half; bring up spot* C	(Page 67)
Cue 48	**Alfie:** "... he's home before dark!" *Fade to black-out*	(Page 68)

EFFECTS PLOT

ACT I

Cue 1 To open (Page 1)
Music: Gracie Fields singing "Sally"; gradually fade out

Cue 2 During black-out on page 7 (Page 7)
Sound of a baby crying

Cue 3 **Edie** and **Dad** smile at each other (Page 11)
Music

Cue 4 **Maurice** smiles to himself (Page 19)
Music; distant sound of birds and kids playing and laughing

Cue 5 **Alfie** runs off (Page 21)
Bring up factory sounds; cut after two verses of the song

Cue 6 **Maurice** follows **Alan** across L (Page 24)
Bring up factory sounds; dip as lights come up DL

Cue 7 **Edie:** "... losing their jobs, that's all." (Page 24)
Factory hooter

Cue 8 **Edie:** "... I will again!" (Page 26)
Music

ACT II

Cue 9 The **Sally Army** forms a circle on stage (Page 36)
Distant church bells ring out

Cue 10 **Abe** and **Buzz** exit (Page 41)
Music

Cue 11 Lights fade on **Edie** and **Lydia** (Page 44)
Music: wedding recessional (Mendelssohn)

Cue 12 **Joyce**: "... on records of course." (Page 44)
Music: something of Glen Miller

Cue 13 **Doris** and **Alfie** go off to dance; after a moment (Page 45)
Change music to "Love Is the Sweetest Thing"

Cue 14 **Betty** and **Doris** go over to **Edie** (Page 46)
Dip music

Cue 15 **Edie:** "I know, love ... I know." (Page 47)
Cut music

Cue 16 The two couples look across at each other (Page 47)
Heartbeat effect

Cue 17 The two couples embrace (Page 47)
Music: "Love Is the Sweetest Thing"

Cue 18 At the appropriate moment (Page 47)
Cut music

Cue 19 All four walk away laughing (Page 51)
Roar of the cotton mill

Cue 20 **Alan** sits; **Maurice** enters (Page 51)
Dip cotton mill sounds

Cue 21 **Tweedale:** "... I don't want it." (Page 53)
Bring up cotton mill sounds to full

Cue 22 The company freezes (Page 54)
Cut cotton mill sounds

Cue 23 **Lydia:** "And you deserve it, Edie." (Page 55)
Music

Cue 24 **Alfie:** "Eric ...! Eric ...!" (Page 55)
Mist

Cue 25 Lights come up on railway station (Page 56)
Hissing of steam engines; tannoy announcement

Cue 26 **Edie:** "... I'm going to miss you!" (Page 57)
Tannoy announcement as in text, page 57

Cue 27 **Abe** and **Buzz** rush off (Page 57)
A loud hiss of steam from beneath the platform

Cue 28 **Doris:** "... to wave us off." (Page 57)
Sounds of the train moving off; hissing steam and a whistle

Cue 29 **Daft Lizzie:** "It's Alfie, Edie ... it's Alfie." (Page 59)
Sounds of another train departing; hissing steam and whistle

Cue 30 The lights fade (Page 59)
Music: Gracie Fields singing "Wish Me Luck As You Wave Me Goodbye". Fade when **Alfie** *begins to speak*

Cue 31 **Tommy** walks around the stage (Page 63)
Music: "Love Is the Sweetest Thing". Fade when **Tommy** *begins to speak*

Cue 32 **Tommy:** "... in *The Staff and Dragon.*" (Page 64)
Piano music: "Roll out the Barrel"

Cue 33 **Irish Mary:** "... shut your heathen gobs!" (Page 64)
Cut music

Cue 34 **Alfie** walks into the spot c (Page 67)
Soft piano music: "Love Is the Sweetest Thing"

Cue 35 **Alfie:** "... he's home before dark!" (Page 68)
Increase music